NEW DIRECTIONS FOR HIGHER EDUCATION

Martin Kramer
EDITOR-IN-CHIEF

The University's Role in Economic Development: From Research to Outreach

James P. Pappas
University of Oklahoma

EDITOR

Number 97, Spring 1997

JOSSEY-BASS PUBLISHERS
San Francisco

378
U58

THE UNIVERSITY'S ROLE IN ECONOMIC DEVELOPMENT:
FROM RESEARCH TO OUTREACH
James P. Pappas (ed.)
New Directions for Higher Education, no. 97
Volume XXV, Number 1
Martin Kramer, Editor-in-Chief

Microfilm copies of issues and articles are available in 16mm and 35mm, as well as microfiche in 105mm, through University Microfilms Inc., 300 North Zeeb Road, Ann Arbor, Michigan 48106-1346.

ISSN 0271-0560   ISBN 0-7879-9890-7

NEW DIRECTIONS FOR HIGHER EDUCATION is part of The Jossey-Bass Higher and Adult Education Series and is published quarterly by Jossey-Bass Inc., Publishers, 350 Sansome Street, San Francisco, California 94104-1342. Periodicals postage paid at San Francisco, California, and at additional mailing offices. POSTMASTER: Send address changes to New Directions for Higher Education, Jossey-Bass Inc., Publishers, 350 Sansome Street, San Francisco, California 94104-1342.

SUBSCRIPTIONS cost $52.00 for individuals and $79.00 for institutions, agencies, and libraries.

EDITORIAL CORRESPONDENCE should be sent to the Editor-in-Chief, Martin Kramer, 2807 Shasta Road, Berkeley, California 94708-2011.

Cover photograph and random dot by Richard Blair/Color & Light © 1990.

Jossey-Bass Web address: http://www.josseybass.com

TCF Manufactured in the United States of America on Lyons Falls Pathfinder Tradebook. This paper is acid-free and 100 percent totally chlorine-free.

CONTENTS

EDITOR'S NOTES

The editor's conceptualization of this volume came out of his experiences in working with the American Economic Development Council (AEDC) to provide certification for professional economic developers and from the very positive responses he received from state and business leaders for conducting an international petroleum conference that created worldwide opportunities for regional energy companies. Now, nearly two years later, the final reading of the chapters prior to submission of the manuscript occurred while the editor was traveling back from the third annual conference on higher education, research, and training for the United States, Mexico, and Canada. The juxtaposition of the final reading and the conference presentations—made by business CEOs, university presidents, and key government officials—was intriguing. This was because the recurring theme of the conference was that higher education institutions are critical in strengthening the economic competitiveness of their regions.

During the conference, numerous case examples were given of how universities from the three countries had fostered local business development. Speaker after speaker insisted that the future for knowledge- and technology-based economies will be related to the ability to harness the research and educational resources of colleges and universities. Interestingly, the strongest supporters of this concept were not the educators but rather the business and government leaders. These presentations have been echoed in a variety of recent public forums, especially in the United States, where predictions are that the future of our economy will not be in labor-intensive manufacturing but in knowledge-based economic development (Pritchett, 1995).

At the same time that increased attention is being given to the role of universities in economic development and global competitiveness, state and land-grant universities are seeking to reinvent their outreach missions. This is in response to legislative and constituency concerns that major universities, in seeking to become basic research centers, may have forgotten their role in contributing to the well-being of their states (Votruba, 1993; McGrath, 1994). A major component of the outreach reemphasis is supporting economic development. Many current educational leaders suggest that we need contemporary versions of agricultural and engineering extension. As a result, continuing education, extension, technology transfer, and other outreach offices in universities are now refocusing or giving greater attention to providing direct services for economic development.

Most of the discussions around economic development tend to be generic and philosophical. Everyone seems to agree on the importance of the outreach role that universities can play in regional economic development; however, there are few clear models as to how the academy can organize itself to indeed

1

become an engine of economic development. Although there are segments of the university that have long been involved with such efforts, the maturing of the professional field of economic development suggested the need for a volume that could bring together the thinking of university administrators, discipline-focused faculty, and economic development professionals to explore ideas and models of how the two trends can come together. The editor is excited that the resulting volume formulates a map that institutions can use to strengthen their campuses' economic development efforts.

In Chapter One, Sherman Wyman creates a context for the interaction between economic development professionals, universities, and the different types of community economic development activities. He proposes the concept of *economic wellness* as a broad comprehensive approach to economic development and suggests how universities' instructional and analytical capabilities will be needed to meet the financial needs of communities. He discusses the challenges of refocusing "university types" to deal with real-life economic problems and how these administrators might redirect academic resources toward meaningful partnerships with public and private entities to solve those problems.

Mary Walshok provides an interesting extension of how to address the issues Wyman presents (Chapter Two). She gives a thoughtful and well-documented analysis of how universities can appropriately contribute to economic development by creating knowledge-linking activities to enhance technology commercialization, community change, and the enhancement of competencies for workers and professionals. Walshok is particularly helpful in identifying the unique roles that universities can play in economic development and gives as an example the effect of her institution's CONNECT program—a partnership between the university and the community that supports entrepreneurial companies—on her region.

In Chapter Three, Gary Matkin defines how the various offices that deal with outreach and economic development can be organized to respond to linkages between the campus and the community. He provides an effective way of conceptualizing continuing education and technology transfer offices and how they relate to the university's role in economic development. He is particularly concerned with defining factors and organizational models for enhancing organizational capacity and culture in universities as they become involved in outreach and economic development. He creates a model for organizing university "soft and hard" technology transfer efforts as higher education institutions struggle with creating a match between the needs of external groups and the loosely federated organizational units that make up a modern university.

James Ryan and Arthur Heim provide specific examples of how some of the units that Matkin has discussed actually engage in technology and economic development liaison efforts (Chapter Four). Their examples come out of experiences at Penn State University in developing partnerships between corporations and universities through such activities as the total quality management project with DuPont, the Benjamin Franklin Technology Center program, the Centre County Industrial Development Corporation, and the Small Industry/Plastics Technology Center. As a result of their experiences, Ryan and Heim describe characteristics of successful partnerships between university outreach and community economic development.

In Chapter Five, economist Will Clark suggests that the evolution of a global information economy requires that universities use new technologies to enhance their regional economic development. He argues that the rapid transition from local or regional to international economies demands that universities embrace new technologies to provide the needed information for their nonuniversity partners to be globally competitive. Technology provides the opportunity for a university to partner with nearly any company based anywhere in the world.

At the same time that Clark is identifying opportunities in international economic development, Usnick, Shove, and Gissy are suggesting ways that universities can prepare for working with their local communities (Chapter Six). They convey a relatively broad view of what community development must be in order to enhance economic competitiveness and illustrate the university as a partner in contexts such as small business development centers, Economic Development Administration university centers, NASA technical assistance centers, USDA extension services, and formal university community development resource offices. They provide case examples of how such university resource centers can be managing partners in bringing together campus resources and local municipalities.

A variation of the work of community resource centers in larger universities is provided by Jerry Young as he describes how local economic development can be enhanced by partnerships with community colleges (Chapter Seven). Young suggests that one of the major roles of the community college has been to strengthen local economic development through workplace-based education, tailored training programs for local industries, job training and retraining, and the development of local business networks. A professional economic developer and a community college president, Young emphasizes the broker and mediating roles of a community college.

Whereas the other authors discuss economic development from an institutional or higher education perspective, Mark Waterhouse draws on his expertise as a professional in the field (Chapter Eight). As a certified economic developer, president of an economic development consulting firm, and former chair of the AEDC, Waterhouse authoritatively discusses the professionalization of the economic development field. He argues that one of the ways that colleges and universities can make a strong contribution to the field is to provide relevant education. By identifying qualified instructors, designing effective degree and lifelong education curricula, and working with state departments of economic development or commerce, colleges and universities provide educational opportunities of paramount importance to economic development professionals. Thus, colleges and universities partner with their external constituencies best when they educate professionals who will carry on the economic development efforts of their communities.

The final chapter develops a series of concepts of how continuing higher educators can facilitate the linkage of university resources with government and industry to foster economic development. The authors' recommendations come from previous writings but are cast within an example of a series of international aviation conferences. This and the preceding chapters clearly demonstrate that higher education institutions with well-defined outreach missions can be key partners in the economic development enterprise.

James P. Pappas
Editor

References

McGrath, P. Comments at the National Association of State Universities and Land Grant Colleges Commission on Outreach and Technology Transfer Conference, Minneapolis, Minn., June 1994.

Pritchett, P. *New Work Habits for a Radically Changing World.* Dallas, Tex.: Pritchett & Associates, Inc., 1995.

Votruba, J. C. "The Future of Land Grant Universities." Presentation at the Oregon State University Extension Service annual conference, Pullman, Oreg., Dec. 1993.

JAMES P. PAPPAS is vice provost for outreach and distance education and dean of the College of Continuing Education at the University of Oklahoma.

Continuing higher education is called upon to become both a catalytic and integrative force on campus to promote a more comprehensive approach to economic development.

A New Vision for Continuing Higher Education: Creating Economic Wellness

Sherman M. Wyman

The theory and practice of economic development has been significantly affected by a number of economic and social imperatives over the past forty years. This chapter briefly reviews this history and applies its lessons toward a more comprehensive vision of economic development in continuing higher education.

Shifts in Policy and Tactics

Economic development among state and local entities in the past several decades has experienced at least three distinguishable emphases, or waves, in policy and tactics (Ross and Friedman, 1991). The first approach preceded World War II and was generally known as *smokestack chasing*. Initially, this approach worked well for southern states and communities, which touted cheap labor, land, and low taxes. However, the northern states successfully counterattacked with tax abatements, training programs, and other public assistance and subsidy programs. This emphasis is still common in many state and local economic development programs although it typically comprises only one part of an overall strategy that focuses on the needs of existing businesses and their employees.

The second wave of the 1970s brought introspection. Efforts were mounted to help local businesses become global competitors. U.S. trade policies, quality products from Japan and Western Europe, and low-cost, labor-intensive items from the Far East accounted for an increasing share of American consumption. The United States woke up to major deficits in workforce skills, technology accessibility, modernization, and new product capital.

NEW DIRECTIONS FOR HIGHER EDUCATION, no. 97, Spring 1997 © Jossey-Bass Publishers

Some states and localities, notably in the Northeast, responded to this shift in approach with foresight. Industrial recruitment was given a lesser priority. The research of MIT's David Birch and others demonstrated that small businesses, not the Fortune 500, were the largest employers. This, in turn, concentrated tactics on small business retention and expansion.

The third wave built on the local involvement and decentralization foci of the second. Walt Plosila proposed eight elements as keys to incorporate an effective, contemporary effort. Many of these elements carry considerable salience for a more comprehensive role for continuing higher education in economic development. They are

1. Build networks and consortia
2. Establish local intermediaries
3. Create wholesale services and programs
4. Require leverage and commitment
5. Make policies and programs comprehensive
6. Generate competition
7. Fill gaps and change behavior
8. Invest; don't grant [Plosila, 1990, p. 12]

This new perspective casts local and state governments, nonprofit corporations, and foundations as facilitators rather than as sole providers. As such, they can act as partners among themselves and with continuing higher educators to enable and promote economic development opportunities through access to capital and nontaxable debt.

Imperatives in the Private Sector

During the past two decades, the shadow of recession has rolled irregularly but inevitably over many communities across the country. The memory of the rust belt 1970s and subsequent decline in major cities of the South has prompted the corporate sector to reexamine its role and relationship to government. Uncertainty over the return from investments in deteriorating urban centers, tax reform, and an increasingly underskilled workforce also has contributed significantly to the private sector's interest in risk-sharing with public development agencies. This reexamination has sparked a new era of private-sector social consciousness and commitment to urban problems. Four principles characterize this current period.

- Committing government resources only where and when real demand exists, an event best demonstrated by the willingness of public and private recipients to share costs.
- Encouraging competition among both public and private providers.
- Leveraging resources, often in formal partnerships, rather than providing sole support.

- Building in feedback for genuine accountability. Do the cost-sharing recipients use the service products? Are they willing subsequently to reinvest? [Ross and Friedman, 1991, pp. 133–134]

While the shift in service delivery orientation from direct responsibility to oversight and collaboration was confronting economic development agencies, other economic imperatives were emerging in the private sector that encouraged a propensity to partner with public and nonprofit agencies. Workforce improvement became a major agenda item among many corporate leaders. The logic of this new attitude, in simplified terms, is that economic vitality is linked to jobs that are dependent on educated citizens working in well-serviced, modern cities that are dependent on a large portion of their tax revenues from those who provide the jobs. The resulting *we are all in it together* mentality has accelerated collaboration among many corporations, foundations, and public agencies to halt urban decline and enhance business opportunities (Davis, 1986).

Our De-Skilling Workforce

As part of this brief history of economic development, several compelling workforce realities must be outlined. First, between 1970 and 1990 unemployment has more than doubled for those with less than four years of high school and for those with high school diplomas (U.S. Dept. of Commerce, 1994).

Peter Drucker sees sober prospects for this group and asserts that "for the foreseeable future, business will remain the largest employer of the poorly schooled. But these business jobs no longer represent the opportunity they did a hundred years ago; they have become dead ends" (Drucker, 1994, p. 184).

It is generally believed that beyond the poorly educated, several million workers are structurally unemployed. Moreover, estimates reveal that ten to fifteen million manufacturing jobs will be lost during the next decade due to foreign competition. Many of those who are displaced will not find reemployment easily without extensive education and retraining.

For most of the past three decades, the private sector has made substantial investments in worker training hoping to ameliorate the skill deficit. However, the total effort by both public and private sectors is still considerably less than our major international competitors (Blatt and Osterman, 1993). And lately, shrinking profit margins, downsizing, and ever-increasing global competition have forced many training directors to admit that diminished training budgets mean devoting most of their effort to skilled workers who are in a position to add the most value to the firm's products.

The New Economic Development: Economic Wellness

Given these emerging challenges to our economy, a new, more comprehensive approach to economic development is imperative; namely, "economic wellness." And, if continuing higher education programs wish to be major players in this enterprise, many significant shifts in delivery and style will be critical. Before treating this issue, let us consider some of the key elements of economic wellness.

First, educational strategies must focus on long-term workforce development as well as the immediate training needs of employees; that is, on careers as well as jobs. Of late there have been major improvements in productivity and efficiency in a number of key industries. Management salaries have increased accordingly. Many categories of workers, particularly those in low-value-added positions, have not realized concomitant wage increases. Accelerated increases in benefit costs and the relatively new constant of ever-increasing global competition account for a portion of the loss. But the prospect for major wage gains for U.S. workers, particularly those with no or limited skills, is bleak. To increase fundamental economic wellness in the current global economic environment means a shift in workforce education, so that it provides ongoing career development rather than just a quick fix for a specific competence for new job requirements or the latest technological innovation.

A career development emphasis requires that continuing higher educators must advocate for an extensive and extended commitment to long-term career development programs. This will require actively promoting an ethic that links continuing education and others with a variety of community-based educational providers for the provision of ongoing career training. An example of such a partnership has been successfully instituted in South Dakota, where South Dakota University and the city of Pierre and Pierre's Capital University Center (some two hundred miles apart) have partnered to introduce associate's degree programs, short courses, and a trained cadre of four hundred adjunct faculty competent in adult learning theory and techniques. In the early 1980s, Pierre and the surrounding rural region experienced a severe economic downturn. Economic survival was dependent on providing access to postsecondary education in order to stimulate industrial growth.

As a result, local citizens formed the Capital University Center to contract with existing institutions for offerings in targeted disciplines (primarily business and nursing) and on-site instruction in a centralized, community location. With financial support from the Fund for the Improvement of Post-Secondary Education (FIPSE), course offerings were initiated, allowing the rural region to determine and obtain education from the college best able to serve their needs. A primary key to the success of the model was the emphasis on a localized approach for program determination, facilities, program coordination, and faculty.

In addition, organizers were able to identify areas of significance for replication: a need for total community involvement and commitment; a need for institutional expertise in off-campus delivery; a high level of trust between the partners; a strong marketing approach; the use of adult learning principles and techniques as well as training of instructors; and a view of the project as a business venture. As a highly successful venture, a critical community need in Pierre has been met through this long-term, long-distance union (Audley and Thompson, 1991).

To develop an effective career development program, it is important that local leaders and educational providers understand the difference between what the businesses of a community produce and what the occupations in its workforce actually do. A career development emphasis requires analyzing the occupational skills of the existing workforce and, where necessary, reeducating them to attract new industries and to increase growth among existing ones.

Fort Worth, Texas, for example, has a large cadre of skilled aerospace engineers and technicians, many of whom have been displaced by recent defense cutbacks. These individuals have demonstrated skills in designing and fabricating airplanes. However, these same skills, with appropriate transfer training, can be employed in a variety of advanced manufacturing careers ranging from appliances to recreational and medical equipment. Such an approach makes analyzing *and* training for career skills a critical partner of the more established processes for targeting new or redeveloped industries (Thompson and others, 1995).

In addition to a pervasive, community-based commitment to career development backed by a solid system of K–12 through postsecondary education, another critical element of economic wellness is infrastructure. The most creative strategies for expansion of existing firms or attraction of new businesses will simply not materialize without dependable utility services and a well-maintained system of transportation. The economic wellness efforts of many communities, large and small, are seriously hampered by ill-maintained infrastructure. Moreover, given the current dominant political ideology, the treasury of the federal government will no longer be available to shoulder a large portion of the cost of upgrading a sewage or water system or revitalizing a central business district. As with other elements of economic wellness, the burden of achievement now rests largely on each community. Those that achieve will be willing to invest for the long-term in workforce education as well as infrastructure.

Beyond these elements, strategies that create value-added employment opportunities from local products are also essential. The value-added process has been characterized as "plugging the leaky bucket." Mary Simon Leuci argues that communities must not only plug leaks with import substitution—making products locally that were previously imported—but by expanding water already in the bucket "by adding value to products already produced in the community. Additional processing adds value and brings money into the community when the product leaves for its market. Most dependent economies export raw products and import finished products for a significantly higher price" (Simon Leuci, 1988, p. 8).

A final element in the economic wellness model is one that is well recognized in adult education theory: the identification and nurture of leaders and resident participants both at the community and, in larger cities, neighborhood level. In developing a theory of adult continuing education programming, Edgar J. Boone proposes that in identifying learning needs "the general idea is that the adult educator, the identified target public leaders and their followers become intensively involved in collaborative identification, assessment and analysis of those publics" (Boone, 1985, pp. 113–114).

Creating opportunities for economic wellness first requires assisting communities and neighborhoods to diagnose their own workforce and physical development needs. The theory guiding this process is one that puts the client (for example, the community) in control of the agenda. That is, leaders and residents define their development objectives in concert with adult educators who provide workforce and economic data to assist in the need assessment and objective-setting process. In addition, assistance in the development of response strategies to meet both physical and career development needs should be provided upon request.

To sum up, a comprehensive approach to economic wellness includes analysis of workforce occupational skills as well as industrial and economic studies; ongoing education and training for careers by both public and private providers to enhance areas of occupational skill strength and to fill gaps; maintenance of viable utility, transportation, and educational systems; generation of value-added employment opportunities from local products; and a long-term commitment to community or neighborhood clients.

Partnerships: A Critical Nexus

Formal and informal partnering with a variety of other community entities ensures not just extended resources but a broad base of economic, political, and social support for economic wellness. Formal partnerships typically offer both public- and private-sector creativity, energy, and influence as well as funds and materials. They are not without risks, but careful attention to the manner in which they are organized can deter many problems. For example, the what's-in-it-for-me mentality can be modified by thoughtful attention to broad representation of the needs and interests of all affected parties.

The history of partnerships suggests there are at least four types of community organizations that, when thoughtfully orchestrated, can collaborate effectively when partnered with universities and public agencies. These include issue forums, foundations, civic and business groups, and partnership management organizations. Each of these types is not always formally involved in every partnership, but it would be hard to envision a successful effort that did not feature some level of involvement from at least two of the four.

Issue forums encourage citizen participation and education. Examples range from neighborhood associations and church-based discussion groups to communitywide organizations such as the League of Women Voters and citizen research and planning organizations. Study and research information, often distributed through continuing education units of local universities, can enhance the open debate these organizations strive to foster.

Historically, the principal contribution from foundations to partnership efforts has been money. But increasingly, the staffs of local and national foundations are becoming directly involved in planning and implementation activities.

This enables them to monitor the effect of their funds and to provide their own expertise where appropriate. The Kettering Foundation, also referenced in Chapter Seven, has provided funds and process facilitators to several midwestern cities to create new relationships between federal, state, and local governments and the private sector.

Foundations typically fall into three groups. The Cleveland Foundation is an example of a *community foundation* with a substantial reputation as a local mover and shaker. It has provided the initiative in Cleveland for bringing together many local parties, including Cleveland State University, to develop collaborative solutions to problems of criminal justice and health care. *Corporate foundations* usually have a national focus for giving, as with the American Petrofina Foundation and the LTV Foundation. Even with national funds, access and attention are gained more easily by causes located in the region in which the foundation is established. *Local private foundations* typically focus on local needs and fund projects of specific emphasis. Examples include the Meadows Foundation of Dallas, a private foundation with a local and statewide project emphasis, and the Tandy Foundation of Fort Worth, which regularly contributes to a variety of events and projects in the Dallas-Fort Worth area.

In smaller and medium-sized communities, *civic business groups* are typically organized and supported by individuals representing all sizes of local businesses. Chambers of commerce and downtown business associations often serve this purpose. In larger cities with multiple corporate headquarters and branch offices, top executives of the firms often create their own organizations. These "CEO clubs" have often been accused of an elitist, closed-door approach to downtown projects with no real concern for the physical and social dimensions of existing neighborhoods. Although the charge may be accurate in some cases, an effective response has been not to alienate the energy and resources represented by these groups but rather to insist on a collaborative process with a broad, diverse base of participation.

Whereas public forums educate and stimulate, business groups promote and support, and foundations fund and facilitate, *partnership management organizations* take the responsibility on a workaday basis for implementation. For smaller projects, management may be provided by a government agency or special-interest organization that may also be the primary funding source. For larger projects, management organizations are typically created by the partnership-planning process to oversee implementation or to actually accomplish the project. In housing and redevelopment partnerships, these organizations are often nonprofit corporations with small professional staffs who are housing generalists. Or the management role may be assumed by a development corporation or investor group with expertise in design, finance, marketing, and legal matters. There are important advantages and disadvantages for both types.

Nonprofit corporations usually are successful in maintaining an aura of neutrality and concern for the welfare of all affected parties. However, the time requirements associated with the participative mode of nonprofits may increase the financial and political costs of projects substantially. Moreover, critical private-sector financial support and leadership may be lost if the planning or implementation stages are prolonged.

Given their commitment to profit, developers and investors acting as managers inevitably attract criticism and occasionally organized political resistance from individuals adversely affected by the project. Special-interest groups also may rebel where their particular concern—aging, homelessness, the environment, or their neighborhoods—is threatened by the profit-driven decisions of the developer or investors.

Higher education representatives should be cautious about accepting a partnership-management role unless the execution of the partnership mission is clearly driven by the university. As later illustrations will suggest, these typically are collaborations where the scientific, technological, or other expertise of the university is the engine for the enterprise.

Style for Economic Wellness

Economic wellness calls for an approach to continuing higher education where the locus of the client is the workforce of a particular community or neighborhood. The focus, or process, involves on-site collaborative strategic planning and partnership development for both physical and human capital development with resident clients and representatives of local firms, governments, chambers of commerce, nonprofits, and other appropriate groups. Such an approach requires a delivery style that is largely mobile rather than campus based.

To address objectives, funds must typically be generated from both the clients and a variety of public, foundation, and private sources. The pursuit of economic wellness typically will not generate front-end revenues. Campus support for the diagnostic and planning stages generally will be necessary until some combination of private or public grants and client support can be realized.

To optimize their effectiveness, continuing higher educators must also generate sufficient support on campus so that both the educational and analytic-research talents of faculty are available to their clients' needs. Examples might include linking science and engineering faculty and their students to the technology problems faced by a local firm or arranging for the provision of economic base or occupational analysis assistance from the economics department. Historically, this has not been a typical mission for many campus continuing higher education units.

Involvement of teams of faculty and students to assist with business and development problems—and to learn from the process—has become an established norm in many professional schools of social work, business, public affairs, health, and engineering. It is important to recognize that there are often thick walls between and within academic schools and departments. Continuing higher education professionals working to build economic potential are in a unique, unattached position to breach these barriers and to provide opportunities for faculty-student community projects and the creation of teams within and across departmental lines.

An interesting illustration is provided by the CONNECT program at the University of California at San Diego, where effective economic linkages to the community emphasize basic rather than applied research. Further described in Chapter Two, this effort was planned by the director of the local economic development corporation, the deans of extension and engineering, and several business leaders. The program includes educational and informational services from university faculty researchers to a variety of entrepreneurial high-technology companies as well as the cultivation of local investors who have provided start-up capital for new technology initiatives. A scientific advisory board of distinguished faculty connects university and industry staff and provides the staff with linkages to other faculty who can be recruited to offer advising assistance (Walshok, 1994).

As might be expected from innovative strategies, not all attempts to link the research capabilities of universities to the economic needs of their communities have readily achieved success. Johns Hopkins, the largest single receiver of federal funds for research, has not experienced overnight success with its $16 million Triad Technology Center. The main problem has been identified as a void of innovative commercial capability at the university. Harvard has had better luck with Medical Science Partners, from whom the university successfully has received $26.5 million from nine investors. And the University of Chicago has successfully raised $8.5 million from four investors to establish Argonne National Laboratories (Feldman, 1994).

Conclusion

Practitioners of economic wellness should be proficient in the skills and operation modes common to the textbooks for continuing higher education and community development—and then some. Some major operational and skill emphases of traditional approaches to continuing higher education can be contrasted with those proposed here, as shown in Table 1.1.

To sum up, economic wellness requires a continuing education commitment to engage the full range of the university's instructional and analytical capabilities to meet the needs of communities, neighborhoods, and even regional associations. This does not mean the radical restructuring of continuing higher education units, although in many cases it will call for a commitment to a more comprehensive mission by the head of the continuing education unit with solid support from key university administrators. Also critical will be the recruitment of qualified staff who can relate effectively to socially and economically diverse community groups and who can engage and excite faculty and students from many disciplines in applied research and training project opportunities.

Challenges for agents of economic wellness will be many. On campus they include coping with organizational and disciplinary myopia and a research

Table 1.1. Higher Education's Approach to Economic Wellness

Traditional	Focus on Economic Potential
Operational Emphasis	
Campus-based	Community-based
Fee support	University, grant investor, and fee support
Defined time period	Long-term, often undefined period
Select faculty as instructors	Many faculty and student teaching resources
Students from dispersed locations	Clients from a specific community or neighborhood
Skill Emphases	
Promotion, marketing, and recruitment	Partnership, grant, and investor development
Job and leisure training	Career counseling and training
Classroom instruction	Group facilitation and brokering

reward system heavily biased toward academic, publishable research; being seen as a threatening presence to other outreach efforts often located in and supported by academic units; and being the recipient of an outmoded disdain by some faculty for continuing education and its practitioners. Off campus, these agents will encounter those who view them as meddling university types unable to understand real problems; endless requests for unfunded assistance; and complaints of inappropriate competition from private consultants and community organizations offering similar services.

But the opportunities far exceed the risks. Funneling a wide spectrum of university resources into constructive community relationships will both expand and solidify the political and social reputation of the institution as well as the continuing higher education function. Most important, it will provide community and neighborhood clients with the fuel vital to the realization of their economic potential.

Note

Professors Wilbur Thompson and James Kunde have been important co-conspirators in the development of the concept of economic wellness.

References

Audley, B., and Thompson, T. A. "University and Community Partnership: Access and Economic Development in Rural America." Paper presented at the Conference of the American Association of Colleges and Universities, Kansas City, June 1991.

Blatt, R., and Osterman, P. *A National Policy for Workplace Training.* Washington, D.C.: Economic Policy Institute, 1993.

Boone, E. J. *Developing Programs in Adult Education.* Englewood Cliffs, N.J.: Prentice Hall, 1985.

Davis, P. (ed.). *Public Private Partnerships: Improving Urban Life.* New York: Academy of Political Science, 1986.

Drucker, P. F. *The New Realities: In Government and Politics, In Economics and Business, In Society and World View.* New York: Harper Business, 1994.

Feldman, M. P. "The University and Economic Development: The Case of Johns Hopkins and Baltimore." *Economic Development Quarterly,* 1994, *8* (1), 67–76.

Plosila, W. "Technology Development: Perspectives on the Third Wave." *Entrepreneurial Economy Review,* Autumn 1990, pp. 11–15.

Ross, D., and Friedman, R. "The Emerging Third Wave: New Economic Development Strategies." In R. S. Foster (ed.), *Local Economic Development: Strategies for a Changing Economy.* Washington, D.C.: International City Management Association, 1991.

Simon Leuci, M. *The Rusty Bucket: Community Economic Development That Makes Sense.* Columbia: Clearinghouse for Community Economic Development, University of Missouri, 1988.

Thompson, W., Hissong, R. V., Kunde, J. E., van Gelder, H., and Wyman, S. M. *The Economic Development in the Fort Worth-Arlington Area: An Occupational-Functional Approach.* Arlington: Center for Economic Development Research and Service, University of Texas, 1995.

U.S. Department of Commerce. *Statistical Abstracts of the U.S. Bureau of Labor Statistics.* U.S. Department of Commerce, 1994.

Walshok, M. L. "Rethinking the Role of Research Universities in Economic Development." *Industry and Higher Education,* Mar. 1994, pp. 8–18.

Additional Resources

Bennett, R. J., and Krebs, G. *Local Economic Development: Public-Private Initiation in Britain and Germany.* New York: Belhaven Press, 1991.

Boone, E. J., Shearon, R. W., White E. E., and Associates. *Serving Personal and Community Needs Through Adult Education.* San Francisco: Jossey-Bass, 1980.

Bradley, B., Schambra, W. A., Barber, B. R., Eberly, D. E., O'Connell, B., and de Oliveira, M. D. "Building Civil Society." *National Civic Review,* 1995, *84* (2), 24–32.

Brockett, R. G. *Continuing Education in the Year 2000.* San Francisco: Jossey-Bass, 1987.

Dressler, D. W., and Newson, R. *Selected Speeches on Adult Education by A. A. Liveright, 1958–1968.* Lewiston, NY: Edwin Mellen, 1992.

Fosler, R. S. (ed.). *Local Economic Development: Strategies for a Changing Economy.* Washington, D. C.: International City Management Association, 1981.

Gessner, Q. H. *Handbook on Continuing Higher Education.* New York: American Council on Education—Macmillan, 1987.

Giegold, W. C., and Grindle, C. R. *In Training: A Practical Management Development.* Belmont, Calif.: Lifetime Learning, 1983.

Griffin, C. *Curriculum Theory in Adult and Lifelong Education.* New York: Nichols, 1983.

Higgens, B. *Economic Development.* New York: Norton, 1968.

Houle, C. O. *Continuing Learning in the Professions.* San Francisco: Jossey-Bass, 1980.

Levy, J. M. *Economic Development Programs for Cities, Counties, and Towns.* New York: Praeger, 1990.

Luke, J. S., Ventriss, C., Reed, B. J., Reed, C. M. *Managing Economic Development: A Guide to State and Local Leadership Strategies.* San Francisco: Jossey-Bass, 1988.

Miller, H. G., and Verduin, J. R., Jr. *The Adult Educator: A Handbook for Staff Development.* Houston: Gulf, 1979.

Mumford, A. *Handbook of Management Development.* Brookfield, Vt.: Gower, 1986.

Munnich, L. W., Jr. *Emerging Principles in State and Local Economic Development: A Benchmarking Tool.* Minneapolis: Hubert H. Humphrey Institute of Public Affairs, University of Minnesota, 1995.

Nixon, B. *New Approaches to Management Development*. Aldershot, Hants, England: Gower, 1981.

Nowlen, P. M. *A New Approach to Continuing Education and the Professions: The Performance Model*. New York: Macmillan, 1988.

Parr, J., and Lampe, D. "A New Paradigm of Leadership: Models for Community Renewal." *National Civic Review*, 1995, *84* (3), 15–22.

Perry, D. C. (ed). *Building the Public City: The Politics, Governance, and Finance of Public Infra-structure*. Thousand Oaks, Calif.: Sage, 1995.

Schein, E. H., and Kommers, D. W. *Professional Education: Some New Directions*. New York: McGraw-Hill, 1972.

"Schools Brief." *The Economist,* Mar. 26, 1994, pp. 85–86.

Senge, P. M., Roberts, C., Ross, R. B., Smith, B. J., and Kleiner, A. *The Fifth Discipline Field-book: Strategies and Tools for Building a Learning Organization*. New York: Doubleday, 1994.

Srinivasan, L. *Tools for Community Participation: A Manual for Training Trainers in Participatory Techniques*. New York: PROWESS/United Nations Development Project, 1990.

Stillman, J. *Making the Connection: Economic Development, Workforce Development, and Urban Poverty*. New York: The Conservation Company, 1994.

U.S. Department of Agriculture. "Business Assistance and Rural Development." Rural Economy Division, Economic Research Service, U.S. Department of Agriculture. Staff Paper No. AGES 9519.

Watson, C. E. *Management Development Through Training*. Menlo Park, Calif.: Addison-Wesley, 1979.

SHERMAN M. WYMAN *is executive director of the Center for Economic Research and Service and associate professor, School of Urban and Public Affairs, the University of Texas at Arlington.*

Regional economic development increasingly depends on access to diverse university capabilities and requires better institutional approaches to putting knowledge to work.

Expanding Roles for Research Universities in Regional Economic Development

Mary Lindenstein Walshok

Research universities, particularly in the United States, have become more central to their societies in the latter part of this century, primarily because they represent the central knowledge resources in those societies. As new knowledge and its applications and absorption increase in significance throughout the economy, in organizations, and for the competency of individuals, those institutions whose primary business is knowledge increase in significance.

Because the United States over the last one hundred years has focused the discovery, development, application, and preservation of all forms of knowledge—scientific, humanistic, and social scientific—in a network of privately and publicly funded research universities, these institutions today are being called upon to participate more actively in knowledge-based regional economic development activities. Universities can appropriately contribute to economic development by developing knowledge-linking activities that enhance technology commercialization, support organizational and community change, and enhance the competencies of workers and professionals.

This chapter offers some examples of the diverse ways in which universities might better organize themselves to serve the society's increasingly complex economic development needs. It proceeds from the assumption that growth and prosperity in a global economy increasingly depend not only on a variety of distinct regional capacities driven by new technological developments coming out of scientific research but also on the policy, business, and cultural issues informed by research in the social sciences and humanities. Thus, any thoughtful discussion of the role of research universities in regional economic development should capture the full range of knowledge development and support activities essential to the process—not just those activities supportive of basic research in science and technology. Manufacturing extension initiatives; continuing education for workers and professionals; technology commercialization programs; public policy centers; and broad, humanistically grounded civic education activities are equally vital to the process.

Multiple Influences on Regional Economic Development

New technologies and the general expansion of the social and industrial uses of knowledge represent the central engine for economic growth in the United States. Studies of regional economic development over the past two decades have focused on the increasingly important interdependencies between research, capital, business services, and public policy in the formation and growth of regions that are coming to be known as *technopolises*—Silicon Valley in California, Route 128 in Massachusetts, the Research Triangle in North Carolina, Silicon Glen and Cambridge in the United Kingdom. Sociological analyses such as that by Rogers and Larsen (1984) on Silicon Valley also emphasize the significance of leadership and social networks, the human infrastructure, as it were, for the development of the shared values and mutual trust critical to communities in adapting to continuous change and innovation in a knowledge economy. Feldman's research (1994) points out that studies of research universities and economic development conclude overwhelmingly that "only with the development of a social structure of innovation can a region hope to gain any payoff for economic growth from proximity to a research university." Research activities alone are not enough (Feldman, 1994, p. 6). The complex array of factors essential to contemporary forms of knowledge-based economic growth suggests the need for a variety of catalytic activities and intellectual resources uniquely suited to the capabilities of research universities. At the most general level they include communitywide understanding of the global context and specific local capabilities affecting regional economic development; management of the technical and social drivers of development; and provision of linking mechanisms and support systems that nurture the "culture" and the social networks essential to knowledge-based economic development.

Table 2.1 summarizes the key knowledge-based activities critical to regional economic development to which research universities can make a unique contribution. These activities include

Table 2.1. Matrix of Knowledge-based Economic Activities

	Supportive Public Opinion and Policy Environment	Assessment of Market Needs	Expansion of Regional Capabilities	Technology Product Development	Organizational Change and Development	Social Networks and Human Capital Development	Encouragement of the "Culture"
Regional economic and social research	X	X	X			X	
Basic and applied research	X	X	X		X	X	X
Technology commercialization			X	X	X	X	X
Workforce development and education					X	X	X
Organizational assessments and management development		X	X	X	X	X	X
Organization of new and interdisciplinary knowledge	X	X	X	X	X	X	
Community forums and leadership briefings		X				X	X
Regional coordination of groups concerned about the role of knowledge	X	X	X		X	X	X

Source: Adapted from Walshok, 1996, p. 144.

- New product development, industry formation, and job creation
- Expansion of regional capabilities in relation to access to advanced professional and management services, sources of capital, marketing, distribution links, quality of life, and so forth
- Assessment of market needs and opportunities
- Assurance of a supportive public policy environment among citizens and officials
- Development of flexible organizations and industries capable of continuous change
- Development of social networks and human capital resources
- Encouragement of a culture of change, innovation, and trust

The matrix also spells out the specific capabilities research universities can call on to assist in addressing these specific challenges. Because of the wide range of competencies in the tenured and adjunct faculty and staff; the availability of libraries, computer centers, and databases; and the large numbers of undergraduate and particularly graduate students, research universities possess much of the raw material essential to putting knowledge to work in these arenas.

Unique Contributions of Research Universities

Research universities are uniquely qualified to discover and develop new knowledge; to fill knowledge gaps in their communities; to provide economic, social, cultural, and organizational trend analyses; to educate and train individuals; and to convene groups concerned about informed, rational discourse on issues of common concern. These capabilities of universities reside in many places within the academy—not just schools of business, engineering, and public policy. However, these capabilities are rarely called upon by the larger society, much less offered by the typically sheltered academic faculty, because to date, universities have not been sufficiently organized and staffed to mobilize their diverse knowledge resources to serve public needs, particularly across the range of issues and at the pace of change characterizing the world today. The matrix suggests universities can contribute to economic development in a variety of important ways, each of which can make essential contributions to comprehensive regional economic development goals.

Economic and social research enables a region to identify strategic assets and important gaps in its industrial base, infrastructure, and geographic and service capabilities. Programs such as the Institute for Public Service at the University of Tennessee and the San Diego Dialogue at the University of California, San Diego are examples of programs that provide ongoing regionally focused research, training, and technical assistance to business and government leadership on issues affecting regional capabilities and opportunities.

Basic and applied research activities at leading universities drive new product development, which in turn gives rise to new companies and new jobs.

Technology transfer and commercialization initiatives are the means by which basic research and the marketplace encounter one another and ideas get transformed into products driving new business formation. Universities that have invested in technology commercialization efforts in addition to basic research have contributed substantially to new industry formation and job creation in their regions.

These activities involve more than patenting and licensing services. They include providing technical assistance, access to business service providers such as attorneys, and connections to sources of capital as well as marketing and distribution links. University-affiliated programs such as IC2 at the University of Texas, Austin; the Ben Franklin Partnership throughout the state of Pennsylvania; business incubators at places such as the University of Utah and the North Carolina Research Park; and the University of California, San Diego's CONNECT program in technology and entrepreneurship are all examples of formal mechanisms to facilitate accelerated technology transfer and commercialization.

Workforce assessments need to go on continuously so that universities can partner with employers in the development of basic and continuing education programs supportive of the skills needed to be economically competitive. Organizational assessments and management development relate to the fact that all organizations must change and adapt to changing economic, demographic, and market conditions. They need assistance in making these transitions and developing new management skills. The University of Vermont has embarked on a relationship with IBM, one of the largest employers in the state, whereby they provide expertise on site to not only deliver education and training but to provide organizational development support and conduct management and workforce analyses essential to ensuring continuous change and competitiveness for this global company.

Organization of new and interdisciplinary knowledge for problem solving and capacity building is essential to providing skill development programs in new and emerging fields of practice. Competency areas such as toxic and hazardous waste management and desktop publishing are needed by industry and require training programs that do not logically come from any single department within the university. Certificate programs through extension divisions and schools of continuing education are providing a vital service here. Universities can also serve as conveners of leadership groups from government, industry, and not-for-profits that are critical to building local support for specific regional development initiatives.

In addition, universities can organize community forums and leadership briefings to introduce new ideas and opportunities for economic development. Without broad public and leadership understanding and support of the complex issues affecting regional development, it is very difficult to make change. Once again, there are examples around the country of university programs that serve this kind of civic education function in communities as diverse as Minneapolis, Wichita, Milwaukee, and San Diego.

Although one can find excellent examples of individual programs on specific campuses supportive of regional economic development, research universities, like many communities, have primarily fragmented, externally funded activities that lack a sufficient range of services and diverse sources of support to have widespread effects. It is important for universities to contribute not only to technology capabilities or workforce readiness, but to enhancement of key regional capabilities and the culture of innovation essential to the forms of economic development characterizing knowledge-based economies operating in a global context. Most campuses have not thought comprehensively about these issues. The activities presented in the matrix, such as technology commercialization supports, regional studies, leadership briefings, community forums, and policy issues all need to be a part of the university's contributions to their region's economic development agenda.

The critical contemporary challenge is that regional economic development efforts need to draw on knowledge resources institutionwide, not just from a single department, division, or school. The economy, the values and capabilities of the community, and the competencies and orientations of individual workers and citizens must all be developing and transforming continuously and simultaneously across a wide range of knowledge issues in the contemporary context of rapid changes in technology and global conditions. If universities are to be critical resources they must create mechanisms that can mobilize knowledge resources campuswide.

Research Universities Can Do Better

Rather than reducing the university challenge to the need for more applied research or vocationally relevant teaching, we need to better develop the institutional mechanisms through which we broker, exchange, develop, organize, and disseminate knowledge to the growing publics for whom it is an increasingly essential resource. Recent history suggests that a knowledge economy with continuous innovations absolutely depends on the unencumbered pursuit of basic research and independent scholarly pursuits.

Experience also suggests that the more effective worker or professional is the person who is broadly educated, with the intellectual flexibility and solid skill base required to continuously adapt to change and learn new things. History and experience tell us time and time again that what is esoteric at one point—Eastern European studies or the sex lives of insects—may be central at another point in time, when ethnic wars or DNA affect our daily lives.

For these reasons, research universities do not need to abandon what they do well. They must continue, even expand their commitment to basic research and the development of expert individuals and fields of study. However, they must also expand programs and develop staff whose primary function is leading or facilitating knowledge linkages across the boundaries now separating knowledge discovery from application, reflection from action, informed discourse from special-interest advocacy. The fundamental problem for research universities, which have such a rich reservoir of information of value to integrated regional development, can be summed up simply. The organizational forms and institutional support and reward systems that have served the expansion of knowledge so well have resulted in fragmented academic disciplines, each with distinct vocabularies and methodologies for developing and communicating about knowledge that are neither easily accessed nor understood by the range of critical contributors to the knowledge-driven economic development process.

Overcoming this lack of fit and difficulty in communicating and collaborating across knowledge boundaries separating spheres of expertise and authority is what needs to be addressed by universities if they are to be truly valuable contributors to regional economic development. In the author's review of research universities making a difference for specific communities through innovative approaches to knowledge linkages, a variety of characteristics common to all the programs, whether focused on economic development, civic discourse, or workforce training, emerged (Walshok, 1995). They include taking steps to ensure a campus culture characterized by

- Highly visible institutionalized and programmatic approaches to outreach and service
- Persons and academic departments within the university that have a flexible view of knowledge and acknowledge the variable sources of relevant expertise inside and outside the academy who are involved in these initiatives
- A desire to learn from nonuniversity sources as well as teach to them
- A genuine commitment to collaboration expressed through broadly representative founding boards and governing committees who set program priorities and formats and identify appropriate sources of expertise
- A commitment to a social dynamic characterized by exchanges, interaction, and networking and thus an acknowledgment that programs must support informal as well as formal activities and a belief that a community needs to be developed

And an organizational structure that supports

- A commitment to flexible and varied formats for information dissemination and knowledge exchange
- An ongoing process of self-evaluation and tracking of program effects, which often means research and evaluation functions within service units
- Multiple sources of funding—private, university, corporate, membership, fees for services—in all the programs to ensure long-term stability
- Components in all of the programs that directly or indirectly enhance the central intellectual preoccupations and resource needs of the university through active faculty and student involvement in a variety of ways

- Programs that are staffed and facilitated by diversely educated full-time professionals who are at home with specific academic and off-campus constituencies and who possess credibility among all the partners in knowledge exchanges, not just higher education professionals
- A significant component of campus leadership support, typically in the person of the provost or the president, associated with every program

The characteristics of the people who lead these various initiatives also reflect a kind of knowledge professional in the university who will become increasingly important. These sorts of professionals, many of whom can be found today working for extension services, research libraries, computer centers, and in academic publishing and radio and television work, can be described as persons who

- Possess advanced academic credentials in the content areas for which they are responsible
- Have some hands-on experience in industry or the community from which to draw in interactions with off-campus constituencies
- Are professionally committed to knowledge-linking roles and academic outreach rather than aspiring to become faculty
- Know how to facilitate problem solving, articulate issues, and identify expertise
- Are skilled at providing linking leadership, facilitating interdisciplinary groups, and serving as conveners in knowledge-related activities [Rosener, 1994]
- Are skilled at written and oral communication
- Are skilled at developing resources and managing projects

Research universities need more programs with these characteristics and more professionals whose primary function is spanning knowledge boundaries between universities and their publics in order to be more effective partners in regional economic development.

A brief example of a program that is making a difference is the University of California, San Diego's CONNECT, a university-community partnership supporting entrepreneurial high-tech companies. CONNECT's emphasis is on new company formation and job creation by providing education, technical assistance, networking, and financial assistance to emerging high-tech enterprises throughout the San Diego region. Funded by membership dues from nearly five hundred high-tech companies, business service providers (such as law firms), and financial institutions, and by underwriting for special events and program fees, CONNECT offers more than sixty programs annually.

They include such things as Springboard, a program for entrepreneurs looking for free legal advice on how to start and fund a new technology or company that in the last year has helped twenty-eight enterprises get started with more than $12 million raised in seed capital. CONNECT's annual International

Corporate Partnership Forum, through which up to thirty emerging companies present their technologies and business plans to potential large company strategic partners, resulted in $600 million in new financing for local companies last year. CONNECT also sponsors numerous seminars on critical technologies and business development issues, as well as luncheons, recognition events, special industry networking groups, a television show, and numerous publications. The program also offers regular research conversations between basic researchers from campus and researchers in industry to increase mutual understanding and networking. Staffed by eight people with relevant technology and business experience, CONNECT continuously links the rich variety of academic, technology, business, and government resources essential to enhancing the regional economy. Its mission, the way it is staffed and governed (a mix of academics and practitioners), its technology content (from biotech to composite materials), its professional content (from law to marketing), and the unique bridging value it represents in a major research university are excellent examples of the previously noted critical cultural, structural, and professional staffing characteristics campuses need to cultivate in order to successfully contribute to regional economic development. Each campus must develop specific approaches to economic development that fit the history and capabilities of both their regions and their institution. But the principles just outlined are replicable from campus to campus. A more detailed description of the key activities and replicable aspects of UCSD CONNECT can be found in Walshok (1994) and Walshok (1995).

Conclusion

Research universities have an increasingly significant role to play in regional economic development if they do three things:

1. Embrace a wider and deeper understanding of the unique character and multiplicity of factors affecting economic development in a knowledge society
2. See their role in society as mobilizing and making accessible campuswide academic resources—from the sciences to the humanities—relevant to the knowledge problems confronting advanced economies
3. Invest politically and financially in the development of institutional mechanisms whose central role is to facilitate, broker, and develop knowledge across the internal boundaries of academic disciplines and across the boundaries currently separating the highly valuable traditional research and teaching programs from the concerns and challenges confronting practitioners and decision makers in the larger society

This means going beyond the development of technology transfer programs, science parks, and special applied degrees, all of which are needed. It means reaffirming what we do well—basic research and liberal arts degree programs. It also means recognizing that new linkages need to be developed campuswide. Such linkages must create bridges between a variety of academic programs and a variety of constituencies in the community. Otherwise, we cannot be sure that the scientific, management, workforce, and cultural climate issues productive of meaningful economic development will be addressed.

References

Feldman, M. P. "The University and Economic Development: The Case of Johns Hopkins and Baltimore." *Economic Development Quarterly,* 1994, *8* (1), 67–76.

Rogers, E. M., and Larsen, J. K. *Silicon Valley Fever: Growth of High Technology Culture.* New York: Basic Books, 1984.

Rosener, J. "Watch for a New Style in the Workplace—'Linking Leadership.'" *Los Angeles Times,* Sept. 11, 1994, p. D2.

Walshok, M. L. "Rethinking the Role of Research Universities in Economic Development." *Industry and Higher Education,* 1994, *8* (1), 8–18.

Walshok, M. L. *Knowledge Without Boundaries: What America's Research Universities Can Do for the Economy, the Workplace, and the Community.* San Francisco: Jossey-Bass, 1995.

Walshok, M. L. "Expanding Roles for U.S. Research Universities in Economic Development." *Industry and Higher Education,* 1996, *10* (3), 144.

MARY LINDENSTEIN WALSHOK is associate vice chancellor and adjunct professor of sociology at the University of California, San Diego.

Understanding how universities have organized noncore functions in continuing education and technology transfer can help university administrators decide how to place economic development activities in an established university organization.

Organizing University Economic Development: Lessons from Continuing Education and Technology Transfer

Gary W. Matkin

This chapter describes how American universities have placed continuing education and technology transfer activities either within the university organizational structure or in relation to it. It also describes the dynamics in universities that affect the way these organizational forms are selected and whether or not they are successful. This description and the implications drawn from it should help university administrators position new or expanding economic development initiatives in the organization or select appropriate external organizational forms to carry them out. The description should also help those outside the university, including potential partners, beneficiaries, and government officials, be better informed and better able to influence university decisions about what part the university should play in economic development and how that part should be played.

Organizational issues surface early when expansion of a university's role in economic development is considered—the activity must be housed somewhere, the people carrying out the activity must report to someone, and they must be paid by some entity. Over the years, universities have developed a wide variety of organizational arrangements both within the traditional academic departmental and disciplinary structures and as auxiliary enterprises. Also, as corporations, universities have the legal ability and an increasing propensity to establish or become involved in a variety of external legal entities, including profit and nonprofit corporations, partnerships, real estate

investment trusts, and loosely organized consortia. This list of possible organizational forms for university-sponsored economic development activities is
thus both long and confusing. The choice of an appropriate form usually is not
limited by internal precedent or legal strictures. Instead, it is influenced by
many considerations. This chapter discusses some of these considerations and
seeks to guide those responsible for university economic development through
the many issues that must be addressed.

The following analysis is based on the author's informal study of continuing education organizations over the last twenty years and a more formal study
of university technology transfer conducted in 1990 (Matkin, 1990). The chapter begins with some definitions and then describes a number of organizational
models for continuing education (CE) and technology transfer, explaining the
advantages and disadvantages of each model. Implications from these descriptions are related to some important large-scale trends in university organizational development, concluding with some advice to university administrators
and those outside the university who are involved in university economic
development efforts.

Definitions

The terms *continuing education, technology transfer,* and *economic development* are
imprecise and have been used to represent very broad and overlapping areas
of activity. Defining these terms therefore requires describing the overlap
among them and limiting definitions to a domain that makes the terms useful
in discussion.

In the professional field of *continuing education,* this term is used to
describe part-time degree programs, noncredit programs, and a variety of
other educational experiences that include those involving informal interactions among teachers and students and even technical assistance programs.
For our purposes, defining CE is less important than describing how it
relates to technology transfer and economic development. Most CE is really
knowledge, rather than technology transfer. Only CE directed at the dissemination of research in technical fields meets my definition of technology
transfer. The relationship of CE to economic development is harder to limit.
Certainly, however, a well-educated and trained workforce is an essential
element in economic development. Therefore any CE directly aimed at helping individuals do better in the workplace, as opposed to providing general
education or cultural enrichment, would fall into the economic development
category.

Technology transfer means the transfer of the results of basic and applied
research to the design, development, production, and commercialization of
new or improved products, services, or processes. University technology
transfer generally refers to the relatively recent activities of technology licensing and other activities directed at creating relations with industry and business development that allow technology licensing and the joint development

of a technology to take place. Technical assistance and industrial liaison programs and some aspects of business incubators and research parks can be considered technology transfer activities. Thus, the term *university technology transfer,* in order to preserve any meaning, should not include the traditional university missions of teaching matriculated students and basic research. By this definition, all university technology transfer activity is also economic development.

Of the three terms being discussed, *economic development* encompasses the widest variety of activities. As it relates to universities, economic development means those activities designed to encourage or promote the economic development of a region, state, or country. I agree with other authors in this volume that for the most part university activities are directed at regional economic development. Universities are often called upon to aid state and local government through programs designed to create new business or attract existing businesses to the region, create jobs, provide technical assistance to local industry, or help in training or retraining people for employment.

In addition to these specific activities, it is increasingly recognized that universities can be instrumental in creating an environment supportive of economic growth by improving the quality of life in an area (Rybczynski, 1995) or by "augment[ing] the social structure of innovation" (Feldman, 1994, p. 68), sometimes called the "innovative milieu" (Saxenian, 1994, pp. 41–43, and Castells and Hall, 1994, p. 246). For the purposes of this chapter, *economic development* will refer primarily to specific activities undertaken by universities that go beyond the teaching and research normally considered to be the institution's core activities.

Models of Continuing Education

University-sponsored continuing education has a relatively long history. A convenient date to mark its beginning is 1915, the year of the first convening of the members of what was to become the National University Extension Association (NUEA). By that time, many large state universities, perhaps led by the University of Wisconsin, had well-established and active extension divisions. Early meetings indicate clearly that the leaders of the extension movement viewed their mission as different from those of their parent institutions but also worthy of full recognition and incorporation into the center of higher education. This different-but-worthy view has been reflected in a number of organizational structures for CE and in a history of debates about the appropriate role of CE in universities. The modern version of these debates has focused on whether university CE should be carried out by a centralized or decentralized unit and assigned to established units of the institution, such as schools, colleges, or departments. A survey of institutions reveals patterns of organization, and a growing body of literature addresses the effectiveness and appropriateness of these patterns. Following is a brief description of four models for organizing CE—the decentralized model, the centralized model, the hybrid model, and the buffer-external model.

The Decentralized Model. In the decentralized model, CE is developed and offered through a number of different units of the university. Professional schools are usually the primary providers of CE in decentralized institutions. Each school determines the nature and extent of its offerings and typically performs many or all of the functions necessary to support such offerings, including marketing, enrollment processing, logistical support, and even record keeping. At the University of Missouri, Columbia, most of the professional schools offer their own CE programs; the School of Business offers executive education, the School of Law offers courses in continuing legal education, and other schools (engineering, library science) also support and staff their own programs. In decentralized institutions, including the University of Missouri, CE in areas not covered by other departments may be offered through an extension or CE office.

The main advantage of the decentralized model is that it keeps the CE function close to the faculty and to departmental interests, thus perhaps encouraging faculty involvement in CE. Faculty and departments can reap the financial rewards of CE and benefit from its many other positive aspects, including closer relationships with professional constituencies and expanded contacts with the community. Decentralized efforts tend to have a greater effect on a narrowly targeted subject area or market niche.

The main disadvantage of the decentralized model is that it tends to serve the needs and desires of the faculty and the department rather than the market. This internal focus often dooms the CE effort to financial failure and to a narrow focus that is fragile and subject to a rapidly changing marketplace. Decentralized functions also tend to be smaller in scale than centralized efforts. Other disadvantages are that the decentralized model is difficult for university administrators to control and coordinate with other efforts; economies of scale in marketing, registration, and other CE functions are difficult to achieve; and the institutional effect of an important educational and service function is diffused. Decentralization usually places CE in the hands of faculty who have many other tasks to do and often lack the skills or dedication necessary to sustain a CE effort. This is particularly a problem when the faculty reward structure does not recognize CE as an important element of faculty roles.

The Centralized Model. In the centralized model, most CE is offered through a unit dedicated to the CE function. Program development, implementation, marketing, and many other operations necessary for carrying out CE, including registration and record keeping, are performed by this single unit. The unit is often called extension or continuing education and is usually controlled by an administrator with the title of director or dean. Even in highly centralized institutions, however, some CE may be carried out by other units, often with the help of the central unit. All but one of the campuses of the University of California system have centralized provisions of CE, although there are small amounts of CE undertaken separately by other units.

The main advantage of the centralized model is that it focuses efforts on CE and makes clear where the responsibility for CE resides. The CE function is more easily controlled and coordinated with other university functions, including alumni relations, development, community relations, and outreach efforts. Economies of scale can be achieved more easily, particularly in marketing, where efforts to market the CE offering can be combined with efforts to promote the institution as a whole. Faculty efforts in CE can be leveraged through the use of CE professionals, who can handle the details of program development, selection, and implementation. A centralized CE unit is usually more market focused and realistic about the market potential of proposed programs. It can more easily create a critical mass of programming and can often generate from internal sources the venture capital needed to initiate new programs.

The main disadvantage of the centralized model is that it can remove the CE function from the faculty and academic departments, thus discouraging faculty involvement in CE. It often results in arguments over control of resources. The centralized CE unit often wants to retain surplus funds to initiate more CE programs whereas academic units want to use some of those surpluses for faculty and departmental projects. The true cost of operating a successful CE program is revealed in centralized units, which can produce debates about how high CE overhead is or should be.

The Hybrid Model. Completely decentralized or centralized models rarely exist; most universities combine the models to some degree. The sharing of the CE function may be along either program or functional lines. Programmatic sharing occurs when certain kinds of programs or certain subject areas are allocated to a centralized or departmental unit. For instance, a university might have a centralized extension unit that does all continuing education except executive education, which is the responsibility of the business school, or alumni CE, which is handled by the alumni relations office. Functional sharing occurs when a centralized CE unit provides support for the CE efforts of other campus units. For instance, the centralized CE unit might help other units market their programs, enroll their students, or prepare course materials. SUNY at Stony Brook is a hybrid model, with the provision of CE divided both programmatically and functionally between an extension unit and professional schools.

Theoretically, if arrangements are carefully worked out, the hybrid model can capture the advantages and minimize the disadvantages of the other two models. In practice, however, hybrid models can be confusing, and jurisdictional disputes can proliferate as market demands change and as the intellectual landscape is altered by technology and events.

The Buffer-External Model. This model conducts CE through an organizational structure outside the institution, often a not-for-profit entity aligned with the institution through ownership of stock or control of the board of directors. Sometimes the entity is associated with a foundation established for fundraising. This model is usually used only for certain kinds of CE activity, not for the full range of CE offered by a university. An example of such an entity is the nonprofit corporation established by a regional entity to foster economic development. An important part of that program is workforce education in targeted areas. As a nonprofit university organization, the entity could engage any higher education institution it chose to deliver the education and could seek funding and pay faculty without regard to university constraints.

The main advantages of the external model are that it can avoid restrictive policies placed on universities and can be more flexible and responsive to the marketplace than internal organizations. For instance, external organizations can be useful when universities are bound by restrictions on faculty compensation or on the use of CE funds earned through the university. In cases in which the institution does not have an established role in CE or its reputation is tarnished, a separate entity might be able to gain greater credibility and establish stronger ties with the community than the university could. Sometimes the buffer-external model can facilitate the formation of partnerships among entities that would have difficulty cooperating in other organizational forms.

There are many disadvantages to the external model. Employees of external organizations often do not enjoy the same benefits as university employees, the use of the name of the university is sometimes a problem, and the university relinquishes some control of the CE function to the external organization. The issue of academic credit can also be problematic, and public relations and the service image of the university may suffer.

Models of Technology Transfer

In contrast to CE, organized university technology transfer is a relatively new phenomenon, dating from the late 1970s. At that time, universities began to be seen as major engines of economic development, particularly in relation to the commercialization of university-produced intellectual property. Central to university technology transfer was the expansion of the technology licensing function, as opposed to the passive patenting function. This function was soon supported by many other technology transfer mechanisms, including research consortia, industrial extension (technical assistance) programs, industrial liaison or affiliates programs, spin-off enterprises, research parks, start-up firm incubators, consultant services, and venture-capital funds.

This proliferation of activity produced a matching proliferation of organizational forms, so many that a categorization scheme is required to describe them. This scheme is pictured in Figure 3.1. The scheme shows the relationship of each organizational form to the central core of the university, which is pictured as the largest circle. Following is a description of each of the organizational forms shown in the figure.

The Integrated Organization. The integrated organization usually is faculty operated, reports to a dean or other academic officer, requires heavy fac-

Figure 3.1. Models for Organizing University Technology Transfer Activity

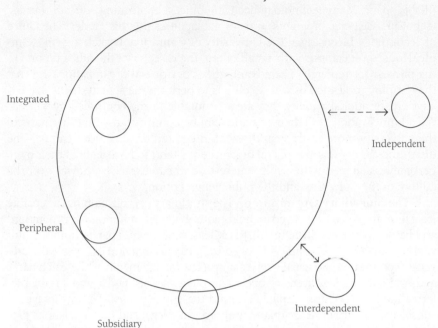

ulty involvement, provides resources to and uses the resources of a department or research unit rather than the university as a whole, and is assigned no or very little separate administrative space. Affiliate programs and research consortia often fall into this category. The industrial liaison program of the College of Engineering of the University of California at Berkeley is a typical example of an integrated organization. It is administered by the dean's office and is housed on campus.

In a very few cases, an integrated organization can be accorded full-fledged status as a university entity. Feller (1994) cites the example of the University of Maryland's Biotechnology Institute, which has coequal status with other UM campuses, its own president, and its own tenure-eligible faculty. The advantages of integrated organizations are that they involve faculty, encourage one-to-one interaction between faculty and industry, and help to shape the culture of the university toward favoring technology transfer. The disadvantages are that the activity of such organizations is rarely controlled or coordinated by the central administration, organizational stability and success are dependent on faculty who have many other tasks to perform, and external constituencies may view the organizations as too self-serving.

The Peripheral Organization. The peripheral organization is not usually operated by faculty or within the departmental structure. Instead, it is most often run by nonfaculty professionals who report to a member of the administrative cadre of the institution, have an administrative staff, and occupy identifiable space. Many technology licensing offices, continuing education units, technical assistance programs, and special facilities use this model. The Office of Technology Licensing at the University of California, Berkeley, is an example. Housed off campus with a staff of ten, the director of the office reports to the provost for research. The advantages of peripheral organizations are that they employ professionals whose job it is to perform the activity, they have relative organizational stability, they are accountable to and controlled by the central administration, and their activities can be coordinated with other parts of the university more easily than those of integrated organizations can be. The disadvantages are that peripheral organizations tend to have a life of their own, become less aligned with faculty interests, and can exercise a power over the culture of the university and the public's perception.

The Subsidiary Organization. The subsidiary organization has a separate legal form in which the university holds equity (usually a nonprofit corporation) and has a governance structure that is at least nominally separate from the university. It interacts frequently with organizations and individuals outside the university community and usually serves only a few faculty members. Research parks and, again, technology licensing operations often use this model, and it is the preferred model for venture-capital and fund-the-gap activities. The advantages of subsidiary organizations are that they afford some legal and public relations protection for the university and can escape university policies that stifle technology transfer activity. For instance, they can compensate professionals on incentive schemes rather than using university-based compensation plans. This model also provides for greater accountability and can serve to buffer university activities from commercial activities. The disadvantages of subsidiary organizations are that the relationship between the organization and the university is often not clear, faculty are even less likely to be involved than in the peripheral model, and the university often has even less control over the organization's operations.

The Interdependent Organization. The interdependent organization is a separate legal entity in which the university has little or no equity and over which the university does not exercise total control but is in some ways dependent on the university. Some alumni organizations and university foundations, such as the Wisconsin Alumni Research Foundation (WARF), and some venture capital funds are representative of this category. Although WARF's bylaws specify that its efforts are dedicated to the purposes of the university, no university officer sits on its board. The university has agreed to provide WARF with rights to its intellectual property in return for research funding. The advantages of interdependent organizations are that, more completely than the previously described types, they separate incompatible activity from the university and buffer the university from negative public relations and charges of undue influence while still allowing the university to exercise some control. The main disadvantage is that much control is relinquished and therefore the risk of embarrassment or scandal may be increased.

The Independent Organization. The independent organization is usually related to the university through contractual or informal arrangements, with the university exercising no control and usually possessing little or no equity in the organization. An example is Research Corporation Technologies, Inc., which contracts with a number of universities to license university-developed technologies. The main advantage of independent organizations is that they provide real separation of the activity from the university and thus usually offer lower risk of all kinds. The disadvantages are that the university usually gives up considerable value in the transaction and can exercise only limited control over the activities of the organization.

Organizational forms fitting within these models are frequently combined to achieve the desired balance among control, buffering, and autonomy. For instance, a subsidiary foundation—perhaps a nonprofit corporation formed to hold ownership of university—developed intellectual property-may own wholly or in part a for-profit independent corporation formed to exploit a technology based on such intellectual property.

Dynamics and Implications

The organizational models just described do not exist in a static relationship to core university functions, but rather change and evolve. These descriptions, therefore, need to be supplemented with some consideration of the dynamics at play and of the models' implications for the larger university organization.

Again, several patterns emerge. The first might be called the *failed integration pattern*. This pattern is recognized by Feller (1994) as a way in which U.S. universities have historically responded to new missions, "accreting" them and then attempting to integrate them with core missions and existing organizational arrangements such as colleges and departments. When these efforts at integration fail, the missions are retained as separate, self-contained, specialized, and often autonomous organizational entities that exist as long as they can attract funding or serve important political constituencies. Much of the infrastructure that has developed to support technology transfer can be seen as fitting this pattern—it was only weakly related to the educational mission, benefited only a few faculty, and violated academic traditions. But because it gave promise of being self-supporting (or even productive of income) and seemed consistent with values held by society, it was allowed to form and grow (Geiger, 1993). Many small-business assistance centers also fit this category; they are first placed in schools of business and then often, when the faculty members do not respond, are given to extension to administer.

Another dynamic might be called the *spin-off*, or *centrifugal*, pattern. This dynamic is characterized by a tendency for the organizational forms to move outward from the university—from the integrated organization to the peripheral organization, from the peripheral to the subsidiary, and so on. This pattern occurs because of a variety of factors.

First, as the functions occurring within the organizations grow and become more important, they are more likely to require nonfaculty professionals to manage and operate them. This happens partly because there is considerable resistance in institutions and among faculty to devoting large amounts of faculty time and energy to noncore functions. And few faculty-reward systems presently recognize noncore activities. Professionals, in their turn, are usually specialists who demand recognition and autonomy and often feel constrained by university rules and processes. For instance, it is logical to compensate technology licensing officers on some incentive scheme, but most universities find such an approach uncomfortable. Second, as the new functions become more market-oriented, complex, differentiated from core functions, or professionalized, the university begins to lose control of the activities and thus has a greater need for the buffering effect provided by subsidiary, interdependent, and independent organizations.

These dynamics combine to create a more fragmented university, in which it becomes increasingly difficult to reconcile disparate missions and to preserve the traditional definition of the role of the university or to define that role in any coherent way at all. They also result in a less faculty-centered institution. Perhaps most important, these dynamics contribute to the emerging *phenomenon of the periphery,* in which what have been considered noncore university functions are beginning to influence and interact with the core in new and sometimes disturbing ways.

Several recent studies and commentaries on university organizational trends have noted this phenomenon. Burton Clark (1995), in his continuing study of innovative universities in Europe, found that the universities that stand out from the rest have four elements in common: (1) an innovative, self-defining idea, (2) an infrastructure with an integrated administrative core, (3) a discretionary funding base, and (4) an innovative developmental periphery. Clark's examples of the elements of this periphery all fall into our definition of economic development. In Clark's view, development of such a periphery is crucial to the success of innovative universities.

Zemsky and Massey (1995) present a less positive view. They see current universities as consisting of "expanding perimeters" and "melting cores," with considerable tension between the two (p. 41). It is well documented that perimeters of universities have been expanding as the institutions assume new roles and seek more resources. This expansion has occurred at the same time that resources for core functions have declined, relative to the costs of those functions, and core functions have not been able to improve productivity or respond appropriately to calls for increased accountability. For example, between 1990 and 1995 university extension revenue at the University of California statewide increased 21 percent (from $110 million to $133 million), and royalty income from intellectual property almost tripled (from $22.5 million to $63.1 million). Over the same period the state of California reduced its support of the universities by almost one-third, from about $1.8 billion to $1.35 billion. This has resulted in a shift and a tension: those along the perimeter now appear less often as venerable citizens of an ancient academy than as the owners and managers of their own enterprises—more concerned with specific outcomes, with the processes of production, and with the kinds of deliverables the market demands. What now worries these entrepreneurs is the center's need to tax the perimeter in order to sustain its core functions, for which there is no longer sufficient revenue. The more that programs, individual faculty, and staff provide for themselves, the more convinced they become that their hard-won earnings are at risk of being siphoned off by a central administration with little discipline and less purpose (Zemsky and Massey, p. 44).

At the extreme, the essential question for those along the perimeter will become whether continued affiliation with a university is worth the tax. A negative answer is not without precedent; there have been a number of cases in which research institutes (Stanford Research Institute, for example), service bureaus, and consulting groups have left their sponsoring universities to take up an independent existence.

Factors to Be Considered in Adopting or Assessing an Organizational Design

As university administrators face the task of organizing economic development activities, they must match the needs of their situation with the characteristics of the organizational models just described. They will also need to consider the dynamics among them. Some of the factors to be kept in mind should be apparent from the preceding descriptions; others emerge from an assessment of the current organizational capacity and culture of the university. Here is a list of those factors and how they might be applied.

Role of the faculty. Some assessment needs to be made of the role the faculty is expected to play in the economic development activity and how consistent this role is with established faculty roles. The larger the role the faculty is expected to play and the more consistent their involvement is with established faculty roles, the more logical some form of integrated model is, absent other factors to the contrary. Little or incompatible faculty involvement argues for organizational forms at or beyond the periphery of the university.

Degree of control. Some university economic activities require a high degree of control by the university, either to assure the success of the activity or to protect the interests of the university. The peripheral organization has the potential for the closest control by the university administration; integrated models usually are controlled by constituent parts of the university rather than its central administration, and subsidiary, interdependent, and independent organizations require by definition some sharing of control with others.

Degree of buffering. This factor is related to degree of control because, beyond the peripheral model, an inverse relationship usually exists between degree of control and degree of buffering—the more control, the less buffering. The protection or buffering afforded by subsidiary, interdependent, and independent forms may be of three kinds: protection from market or financial risk, protection from legal liability or potential litigation, and protection from negative public relations.

Interaction with partners and degree of community involvement. Many forms of economic development involve individuals and organizations outside the university organizational structure, and the degree and nature of their involvement has a significant bearing on the form of organization to be chosen. In some cases, even with anticipated heavy involvement of the community, a university organization of the peripheral or subsidiary kind is appropriate because the university can serve as a neutral convener of groups not used to interacting with each other. In other cases, it is useful to deemphasize university involvement in order to give community groups a sense of ownership and empowerment. For the most part, interdependent or independent organizations are most appropriate for activities requiring significant involvement by outside agencies or groups.

Internal factors. Many other factors, both internal and external to the university, must be taken into account when deciding how to organize university economic development efforts. Because external situations are so varied, it is difficult even to generalize about external factors. Many of the internal factors are also difficult to specify, but they fall into describable categories. *Organizational capacity* is an important general issue. Does the university have the internal capacity to perform the function, or should the function be handled outside the university by some other entity? Can *existing units* within the university administer the activity or will some *new entity* and accompanying infrastructure have to be developed? Is the new activity consistent with the *organizational culture* of the university, or will dissonance with that culture cause it to encounter sabotage, resistance, neglect, or reluctant and condescending support? Does the university have a *history* supportive of and consistent with the new activity, or has some scandal or past difficulty permanently colored institutional perception of that kind of activity? Do any special *financial, management, or risk issues* need to be addressed? For instance, does the university accounting system have the capacity to handle the transaction volume or reporting requirements of the new activity? Will the university subject itself to risks not covered by current institutional insurance programs? Finally, and most important, does the new activity or program have the *commitment of leadership* essential to its success? Few economic development programs will have smooth sailing right from the start. They will encounter problems that only committed leaders can overcome.

Knowledge of regional development. There is a more critical determination university administrators must make, one that can influence the choice of organizational form profoundly but one that also is more important than organizational form. That determination is: How best can economic development be brought to a target region by a university? Too often a university is pressed into economic development activities that cannot succeed because other critical elements of economic development are lacking. For instance, the University of

California, by virtue of its contract for managing the Los Alamos National Laboratory, recently has been asked to promote high-technology industry in northern New Mexico, a sparsely populated area. In the author's view, these efforts are unlikely to succeed.

What is often lacking on the part of both universities and the communities they serve is an understanding of the very complex process of regional economic development. Required is the identification of an appropriate starting point. For instance, the University of California, San Diego CONNECT program, described in Chapter Two of this volume, was created because the business infrastructure in San Diego was not sufficiently developed or sophisticated to support high-technology entrepreneurialism. Once the community had been organized through the CONNECT program, the university had a much more receptive market for its intellectual property and the university research community developed new linkages to the industrial community.

These two examples also illustrate the relationship between technology transfer and economic development. Effective university technology transfer, that is, technology that results in economic development, is only one of several important components of economic development. For instance, as has been the case in northern New Mexico, technology transfer has been effective in creating new, start-up, high-technology businesses, which move away to more urban areas when they become successful. Universities need to learn a great deal about the dynamics of regional development so that they can educate their local communities, adjust expectations to what reasonably can be accomplished, and structure university involvement appropriately, thus avoiding a no-win situation.

Implications for External Groups and Organizations

Perhaps the most important lesson of this discussion for external groups and organizations is that there is no such entity as *the university*. Universities are composed of many organizational units that often have different and even conflicting agendas. An understanding of the relationships among the parts of the university and the dynamics of these relationships can help external groups influence university activities. External groups can help their university partners gain power and avoid internal conflict, they can shoulder their share of the responsibility for activities, and they can avoid pressing universities beyond their capacities and competencies.

As external groups and agencies enter into partnerships and other kinds of arrangements with universities, they need to do their own careful assessment not only of the university as a whole but also of the organizational unit(s) within the university to which they will relate and on which they may depend. Using the guidelines in the preceding section, they need to assess the correctness of the organizational fit of the university entity charged with responsibility for the activity, asking their own questions about the commitment of leadership, the stability and staying power of the organizational unit, and the relationship of the activity to the core activities of the university. Increased knowledge and sophistication on the part of university constituencies about university organization and dynamics can make a significant contribution to the success of regional economic development.

Recent organizational changes in the University of California's technology licensing function illustrate many of these factors and implications. The regents of the University of California established a centralized patent office in the 1960s to control the university's patentable intellectual property. The main functions of the office were to inventory and then protect with patents, when appropriate, inventions and discoveries made by university researchers. As the number of inventions rose and as pressures from the faculty and the public to license and place intellectual property into commercialization mounted, the capability of the staff to handle the work was well exceeded. The regents delegated authority over the office to the president of the university, and the staff of the office was expanded. The emphasis was placed on licensing rather than protecting intellectual property.

In 1989, a new director was hired, and along with a senior vice president, proposed that a nonprofit foundation be formed to handle regents' intellectual property and a for-profit corporation be formed to handle venture capital accumulation and investment. These ideas were dropped after a lengthy controversy prompted primarily by faculty concerns and played out in the press. However, faculty on the nine campuses continued to complain bitterly about the lack of service, even from the expanded office, and the business community complained about the difficulty in doing business with the university. Berkeley and UCLA asked for and were granted permission to start their own campus technology licensing offices. These two were followed by UC San Diego, and UC San Francisco and UC Davis are now in the process of establishing their own offices.

This story, briefly told, is a realistic example of several aspects described throughout this chapter. First, it is clear that the regents' primary concern in the early years was control. Control is most effectively exercised by a centralized unit. As the control function grew, it became a barrier to development, which upset key constituencies. When professionals were hired to serve these constituencies better, they quickly sought release from controls by trying to move from a peripheral organizational form to a subsidiary organizational form, illustrating the centrifugal force postulated earlier. However, the subsidiary form was dropped when it threatened to move the function too far from faculty control. Now the university is trying to locate the function closer to the faculty of each campus. This scenario illustrates the importance of faculty and the conditions under which a decentralized model might be more appropriate.

Conclusion

There can be no doubt that regional economic development activities have become a permanent part of the agenda for American higher education. Those activities are likely to expand in the next few years and become more important in the lives of both universities and the communities they serve. The way in which universities organize such activities will both determine and reflect some fundamental shifts in university organizational structure and a radical redefinition of the role of the university in society. University economic development activities, including continuing education and technology transfer, are now part of the innovative, entrepreneurial, expanding perimeter of higher education, which has a fluid and uneasy relationship with the core and tradition of higher education.

The more successful universities are in performing noncore, nontraditional functions, the more likely they will be able to retain coherent institutional identity in our society—yet the more different that identity will be from the traditional one that has survived since the Middle Ages. Of course, failure at these activities may well precipitate another kind of crisis. In spite of this double bind, those of us on the perimeter are optimistic, confident, and excited about our role in the university community, which we expect to continue far into the future.

References

Castells, M., and Hall, P. *Technopoles of the World.* London: Routledge, 1994.

Clark, B. "Case Studies of Innovative Universities: A Progress Report." Paper prepared for the 17th annual forum of the European Association for Institutional Research, Zurich, Aug. 27–30, 1995.

Feldman, M. P. "The University and Economic Development: The Case of Johns Hopkins University and Baltimore." *Economic Development Quarterly,* 1994, *8* (1), 67–76.

Feller, I. "The University as an Instrument of State and Regional Economic Development:The Rhetoric and Reality of the U.S. Experience." Paper presented at the Center for Economic Policy Research Conference, Stanford University, Mar. 18–20, 1994.

Geiger, R. L. *Research and Relevant Knowledge.* New York: Oxford University Press, 1993.

Matkin, G. W. *Technology Transfer and the University.* New York: Macmillan, 1990.

Rybczynski, W. "The Rise of the College City." *New York Times Magazine,* Sept. 17, 1995, p. 58.

Saxenian, A. *Regional Advantage.* Cambridge, Mass.: Harvard University Press, 1994.

Zemsky, R., and Massey, W. F. "Expanding Perimeters, Melting Cores, and Sticky Functions: Toward an Understanding of Our Current Predicaments." *Change,* 1995, *27* (6), 40–49.

GARY W. MATKIN is associate dean, University Extension, University of California, Berkeley.

Universities are rapidly increasing their involvement with corporations to support economic development.

Promoting Economic Development Through University and Industry Partnerships

James H. Ryan, Arthur A. Heim

Institutions of higher education in America, especially land-grant universities, were founded on the basis of being responsive to the economic well-being of the nation (Walshok, 1995). The vision in creating these resources in service to society was to undertake creative and curiosity-driven research, to provide for the formal education needs of future workers, to transfer technology and knowledge to agricultural and mechanical industries, and to update the skills of the workforce. Over the last hundred years, universities—both public and private—have been actively engaged in broad-based partnerships that have been beneficial both to themselves and the broader constituents they serve.

As universities serve their economic mission, business is experiencing an internationally competitive marketplace, and the explosion of knowledge is influencing all organizations. The application of the latest theories and techniques often means the difference between the success and failure of a business. "Technological and other advances must become part of the mainstream of the economy, and new knowledge must be absorbed by existing enterprises if they are to survive" (Lynton and Elman, 1987, p. 22). The importance of increasing access to information and the rapid adoption of that information is recognized by many corporations in their commitment to process innovation and human resource development. This approach is typified by one major automotive company that has developed a key strategy for future success around the concept of "outlearning the competition."

As we move into the twenty-first century, with increased competition, unanticipated demands and forces, and accelerating change, a significant growth in

NEW DIRECTIONS FOR HIGHER EDUCATION, no. 97, Spring 1997 © Jossey-Bass Publishers

partnerships between universities and business and industry is inevitable. Considering new telecommunications technologies, access to these relationships is no longer bound by geography. Technology has allowed new partnerships to occur across traditional state, national, and international boundaries. A dramatic increase in the interaction between the universities and external constituents is essential to maintain economic well-being in support of business competitiveness.

This chapter briefly presents examples of partnerships, examines the way such partnerships are formed, and discusses the benefits to universities and the corporate world. The examples used are from The Pennsylvania State University, where the authors have more than thirty-five years of combined experience in developing and nurturing these relationships.

Examples of Effective Partnerships

Effective partnerships by universities and industries in support of economic development are formed around mutual needs, market demands, and the potential of value added as a result of teaming. The four cases that follow present different models of such partnerships.

Corporate-University Partnership. The DuPont Corporation and Penn State have enjoyed a longstanding relationship recently enhanced through a mutual interest in total quality management (TQM). The corporation has adopted TQM as the cornerstone of a movement to restructure the company following an era of downsizing and reengineering. The partnership facilitated Penn State's adoption of the TQM philosophy and adaptation of the models developed at DuPont. An additional outcome of the partnership was a communication protocol that enables direct linkage between university and corporate officials in strategic areas of interest. The focus areas include human resource development and continuing education, technology transfer, and the advancement of the TQM relationship. The linkage is made operational through single points of contact in each of the focus areas. The technology transfer points of contact are Randolph Guschl, director of technology acquisition at DuPont, and Arthur Heim, director of the Industrial Research Office at Penn State. The human resource development points of contact are David van Adelsberg, vice president of The Forum at DuPont, and James Ryan, vice president and dean for continuing and distance education at Penn State.

The Heim-Guschl team has taken on the role of technology liaison between the two institutions, each representing the mission and interests of his respective organization. As a function of its recent reengineering strategy, DuPont seeks to acquire relevant technology from sources outside the corporation. The corporation's interest in outsourcing research and development is viewed as an opportunity for a major research-based institution. Effective technology-based linkages, however, demand close attention to the requirements of the industry partner and an awareness of cultural differences within the organizations. The single point of contact and the personal relationship developed between Guschl and Heim have proven to be a successful bridge across corporate and university culture. DuPont and Penn State have successfully launched research and technology-development projects in advanced materials, housing and construction materials research, business, and biotechnology.

The DuPont-Penn State Continuous Quality Improvement Partnership is led by Ted Brown, DuPont's manager of quality and process control, and Louise Sandmeyer, executive director of the Continuous Quality Improvement Center at Penn State. The DuPont-Penn State partnership was forged in 1993 under the nationwide TQM challenge to business and universities. In addition to the technology-transfer linkages just described, the partnership has produced a benchmark workshop for academic quality cosponsored by Penn State and DuPont. The focus was on the academic advising process and attracted representatives from more than twenty universities. In continuing and distance education, the partnership enabled a productive relationship to grow with Forum, Inc. (DuPont's training service provider), to develop jointly a comprehensive response to the corporate training needs. DuPont team members are also involved in an innovative manufacturing engineering program that will revise the engineering curriculum to emphasize the interdependency of design in a business environment.

The products of the DuPont-Penn State relationship are substantial, and the future holds great promise. Teams have been formed in academic and administrative units with individual efforts to design strategies and implement positive changes. The DuPont-Penn State partnership has led to the implementation of a first-of-its-kind, broad-based working agreement that could be crafted only on a foundation of trust and mutual respect.

State Government and University Partnership. The Ben Franklin Partnership Program evolved in an era of recession and degradation of the rust belt industries in Pennsylvania. The program was founded on the premise that universities and industries should partner in an effort to improve the competitive position of the firm through the transfer of technology from the state's universities. The state provides the catalyst for the partnership through funding support and assistance in project development. The program is administered by four geographically dispersed centers located within or adjacent to major research universities in Pennsylvania. The Ben Franklin Program requires a commitment from both industry and university partners in the form of leveraged resources, typically cash from the company, and the commitment of facilities and talent from the university. Since its inception, the program has stimulated the growth of new technology-based firms and helped the state's established manufacturers to adopt new process technologies.

The center's report card is impressive. Since 1983, more than twenty thousand new jobs have been created, more than nine hundred products commercialized and process enhancements implemented, and eleven hundred companies created. Over the course of the program, $250 million of state investment was leveraged with more than $1 billion in private sector, federal, and university support. The program is consistently viewed as a benchmark among the nation's state-supported technology and economic development programs.

The benefits to the university are numerous. For fiscal year 1995, almost $900,000 in Ben Franklin project support came into Penn State. This state investment was matched with an equal amount of private-sector cash. Other investments (equipment, services, and federal funds) totaled more than $3 million. The total value of the program to Penn State alone for fiscal year 1995 was in excess of $4.1 million. The dollar value represents only one element of the program's benefits to the university. Each Ben Franklin project involves a partnership driven by the private sector (a company), and typically includes graduate students working on behalf of the company under the leadership of faculty researchers. The experience gained by the faculty-student combination is invaluable and often leads to an employment opportunity for the student.

Local Community and University Partnership. The Centre County region of Pennsylvania has enjoyed impressive growth and economic stability, due in large part to the role Penn State plays as a catalyst for enterprise development. The partnership formed by the Centre County Industrial Development Corporation (CCIDC) and Penn State has led to the formation of a small business incubator funded in part by the Ben Franklin Partnership Program. The incubator has spawned more than twenty-five businesses, many of which were the result of a university-developed technology, spun out in the form of an enterprise. The incubator is located in the Penn State Research Park, which in itself exemplifies the partnership with the business community.

The Penn State Research Park evolved from a vision to encourage economic development by providing a location and infrastructure adjacent to the university's human and informational resources. Penn State's technology, its economic development and business support services, the small business incubator, and a major state-of-the-art conference facility all reside in the park. In addition, the park houses the Materials Research Institute, a partnership with many of the nation's leading industrial firms, with a mission to bring to commercialization the leading-edge advances in advanced materials. The CCIDC-university partnership enables entrepreneurs to access facilities and support services available for start-up companies. The partnership also enables businesses to link quickly with the matrix of state and federal incentive programs supporting economic development.

The existence of the Penn State Research Park provides the environment for university research to realize commercial potential. Intellect is transformed into enterprise facilitating opportunities for the university community to find productive employment, a training site for student interns, and a living laboratory for collaborative research with industrial partners.

Small Industry-University Partnerships. Northwestern Pennsylvania is home to one of the largest concentrations of plastic parts makers in the nation. Approximately a thousand firms are clustered in the Erie County region along with supporting industries like tool-and-die and materials producers. The industry is deeply concerned about the skill level of its employees and their competitive position in a global economy. A consortium of small firms was formed to address the problem. Penn State Erie, The Behrend College, facilitated the formation of a consortium of companies with common interests and linked with the Ben Franklin Program to form the Plastics Technology Center. The center grew to more than forty corporate members and is currently housed on campus in a fifty-thousand-square-foot laboratory entirely funded by local industry. In addition, the center was awarded a National Institute of Standards and Technology Manufacturing Extension Center designation with annual funding in excess of $3 million.

Penn State-Behrend currently offers a full range of training programs that emerged from the plastics initiative. Students have the option to pursue a bachelor's or master's degree program in plastics and materials technology. Placement rates in these programs are currently at 100 percent. With increasing numbers of graduates employed in local industry, the demand for continuous skill improvement and technology transfer has increased. In response to this demand, the Plastics Technology and Deployment Center evolved with a comprehensive array of technology assets and support services unmatched in the country. The lasting benefits to the university are many, with the focus being a state-of-the-art research and training facility housing the most advanced equipment in the industry. The campus prides itself on the fact that this accomplishment evolved from a partnership with the community, industry, and government. The investment is returned in the form of enhanced employment opportunities for students, a more competitive local industrial base, applied research opportunities for faculty, and significant broad-based funding support.

Types of Relationships

The development of industry-university-government partnerships may take any one of three forms. Most all conform to one of three models: institutionally directed, industry directed, and government catalyzed.

Institutionally directed partnerships are initiatives that are focused on an external constituency. Academic expertise and other unique capacities are targeted to a potential user. This push of technology or knowledge facilitates the transfer of expertise from the university laboratory to the potential user. Technology push occurs when the institution views its intellectual capacity as valuable to the private sector, and a proactive effort is made to target the technology to a receptive market. Universities are often viewed as a reservoir of intellect and often aggressively market technology to potential users in the private sector. If a successful relationship is developed, a partnership is formed that enables the technology to transfer to the user with the right to gain value from it. In addition to the commercial potential resulting from the transfer, the partnership often results in further joint research activities that continue to enhance the value of the relationship. The technology-based relationship often requires a component of ongoing training and continuing education that enables the innovation to take hold in the workplace.

A case for institutionally directed industry-university partnerships is evident in the foundry industry in Pennsylvania. Expertise in the Department of

Environmental Engineering at Penn State was directed to a chronic problem plaguing the industry. Penn State researchers developed a technique for safely disposing of and recycling spent foundry sands. These sands often contain hazardous materials and could not be economically treated and disposed of. The industry was in rapid decline in the state, and the environmental issues would have hastened the industry's end. A series of projects were implemented and resulted in an environmentally friendly method of removing hazardous materials from the sand and recycling the usable material. The foundry sand projects were partially funded by the Ben Franklin Program and a consortium of metal-casting manufacturers. As a result of this multiyear project, the industry has stabilized and is making a comeback in Pennsylvania.

The foundry sand initiative provides an example of a university-directed partnership that effectively links academic, outreach, and funding resources in response to an industry need. In this example, outreach structure and strategy was imbedded within the Research and Technology Transfer Organization (RTTO). The RTTO functions include the Pennsylvania Technical Assistance Program (PENNTAP) serving as the industrial extension service; the Ben Franklin Technology Center providing funding support; and the Industrial Research Office serving as the industry research and technology liaison activity. The RTTO has responsibility to assess the opportunities in industry and match the need with university resources. University-developed technologies with potential application or fit to industry are often showcased to encourage users to link with intellectual capability. The RTTO provides the linkage mechanism that enables the technology to be pushed out to the industry user and the support structure necessary for the innovation to take hold.

Industry-directed partnerships are demand-driven, with the industry partner expressing a need or opportunity. Often expressed as *technology pull*, industry needs are directed to a knowledge base in the university. Technology pull is typically in response to real-time technical needs or opportunities with short-run effects on the industry partner. The university response may be in the form of transferable technology or knowledge. University outreach efforts enable industry users to link with institutional resources through technology transfer, continuing education, and extension mechanisms.

The food-processing industry offers an example of an application of an industry-directed partnership. Food processing remains vital to the Pennsylvania economy, accounting for the largest segment of manufacturing employment in the state. Food processors—the poultry industry, in particular—have a serious workplace safety problem. The work requires a high degree of manual operations with a concentration of tasks involving the hand and wrist. Repetitive-motion injuries are rampant, with carpal tunnel syndrome being a leading cause of worker compensation claims and lost productivity. One major processor in central Pennsylvania claims a 100 percent turnover of workers due to this kind of injury. In this case, the company asked Penn State to investigate the problem. With funding support from the Ben Franklin Program, several research projects were initiated. University researchers in industrial engineering evaluated and improved the work process, eliminating some of the injury-causing tasks. In addition, new tooling was designed to accommodate the operation with consideration given to the limitations of the human hand and wrist. Training programs were employed to assist workers in their understanding of the workplace dangers and the use of newly designed tools and techniques.

Industry-directed partnerships often occur by way of a historic relationship between a company and a university. These relationships may be fostered by strong personal linkages around a focused technical area, the hiring of graduates, recognized faculty research, or other common areas of interest. Traditional linkages tend to have a narrow band width and limited deliverables. University-industry outreach activities and service providers greatly expand the potential of these linkages and relationships. University-based industry outreach centers are the interface mechanism that enables precise linkage to human resource and technology capabilities. Within Penn State, outreach and institutional linkages are structurally defined in the following functional areas: Continuing and Distance Education, the Research and Technology Transfer Organization, and the Cooperative Extension Service.

Government-supported university-industry relationships occur when industry and the university collaborate by way of the catalytic efforts of government. As mentioned earlier, the Ben Franklin Partnership in Pennsylvania provides the example in this arena. In this case, the state, through its policies supporting industrial growth and development, provides the catalyst for technology-based economic improvement by sharing the cost of innovation through encouraging partnerships of industry and universities. The state's investment is leveraged greatly by the industry and university partners' commitment of resources. The value back to the state comes in the form of new jobs created and jobs retained in Pennsylvania industry.

PENNTAP and the Industrial Resource Center Program (IRC) represent additional examples of state-supported initiatives targeting industrial improvement. PENNTAP, housed at Penn State, provides cost-free technical assistance and information services to small manufacturers targeting process improvement and solving problems on the factory floor. The IRC program provides more in-depth assistance in response to product and process design and improvement needs. The IRC often uses university expertise as a problem-solving resource. These programs, when combined with the Ben Franklin initiative, result in a comprehensive package of state government-driven partnership programs that encourage the linkage of industry and universities for the economic well-being of Pennsylvania.

Federally supported and encouraged industry-university relationships also provide incentives for value-added partnerships. The National Science Foundation (NSF) Engineering Research Centers Program and the Industry/University Research Centers Program represent examples of government-encouraged collaborative partnerships between industry and universities. Both programs are intended to be industry-driven with a focus on applied research relevant to industry needs. Technology and knowledge transfer are required deliverables of the programs. These NSF initiatives are largely industry funded and managed through a consortium agreement with the industry partners. The university conducts the research, but the topics are determined by the center members, and results quickly transferred to industry users.

Partnerships between industry, universities, and the government work when the university is a willing and able partner and views the value in the relationship. This is not always the case. All too often, universities fail to understand that industrial partnering and economic development activities are more applied than basic research-oriented and industry-driven. In Pennsylvania, state government views Penn State as a vital asset in its economic development strategy. The state and the university often team, projecting a seamless set of attributes that make an attractive package to an expanding or relocating industry. The partnership works in Pennsylvania because of the university's commitment to economic development, its outreach infrastructure, and its responsiveness.

Characteristics of Successful Partnerships

As stated earlier, characteristics of effective and successful partnerships are formed around the recognition of mutually reinforcing needs and an understanding of the value added as a result of developing a relationship. However, partnerships are not easily formed and are even more challenging to sustain, especially between universities and the corporate world, where the cultures are quite different. The development of partnerships is enhanced when the parties involved understand each other's needs, wants, and expectations.

University needs fall into three categories—support for students, opportunities for faculty, and institutional advancement. Increasing financial aid and assistance to students as well as opportunities for internships, co-ops, placement, and experience in a real-life laboratory are benefits of such a partnership.

Faculty are anxious to apply expertise and test concepts, find new consulting opportunities, and acquire new opportunities for research. The university as an organization benefits from support for faculty and staff and the generation of additional income and public support. Occasionally, university inventions resulting from these partnerships are licensed and provide new sources of income. Also, joint ventures are developed to create new enterprises that can be financially beneficial to both parties.

The needs of the corporate world are different; their requirements are quality, specialized expertise, and assistance that is flexible, responsive, and cost-effective. They may demand confidentiality in these relationships. They also expect a contribution that is directly measurable and affects the bottom line. For business and industry, partnerships need to produce a clear return on investment. This can be measured in the number of jobs saved or created, number of new products or businesses developed, or productivity enhancements. An understanding of the difference in orientation in merging these cultures is an essential element of successful partnership.

The following are characteristics common to successful partnerships:

1. *An understanding of capabilities, expectations, and interests* must be clear to both parties entering into a relationship.
2. *Value-added incentives and outcomes* must be built in and recognized as necessary and desirable for both partners.
3. *A single point of contact* between the university and the corporate partner is important in order to develop effective linkages and communication.
4. Partnerships take time to develop and require *an investment in learning about the organizational culture of the participants.* Through this investment, a better understanding of traditions and values occurs, and trust and communication are enhanced.
5. Successful partnerships must be continually nourished through *an oversight process that ensures that commitments are delivered on time* and that there is prompt follow-up, problem solving, and evaluation.
6. *A formalized outreach structure* must be in place in the university that understands and responds to—as well as seeks—partnership opportunities. Without an appropriate structure, a vision that such partnerships are desirable, and organized strategies to create these opportunities, the development of sustaining partnerships will be inhibited.

Effective partnerships are founded on mutual need, trust, effective communication, and an understanding of the value added for both partners. As we look at the future, partnership activities between colleges and universities and the communities and states they serve will become more widespread. Lynton and Elman have recognized this potential: "The totality of universities represents an enormous potential that could be mobilized if a substantial portion of faculty in a substantial number of these universities were more actively involved in technology transfer and knowledge diffusion" (Lynton and Elman, 1987, p. 24). The challenge will be to make sure these partnerships become nourishing to both and do not dominate or detract from the broader mission and responsibility of colleges and universities.

References

Lynton, E. A., and Elman, S. E. *New Priorities for the University: Meeting Society's Needs for Applied Knowledge and Competent Individuals.* San Francisco: Jossey-Bass, 1987.
Walshok, M. L. *Knowledge Without Boundaries: What America's Research Universities Can Do for the Economy, the Workplace, and the Community.* San Francisco: Jossey-Bass, 1995.

JAMES H. RYAN is vice president and dean for continuing and distance education at The Pennsylvania State University.

ARTHUR A. HEIM is director of the Industrial Research Office at The Pennsylvania State University.

The evolution of a global information economy presents economic developers and education specialists with unprecedented opportunities and challenges.

The Global Information Economy and Its Effect on Local Economic Development

Will Clark

Economic developers and continuing education specialists now practice their crafts in a global economic system. Facing competitive challenges from Europe to the Pacific Rim, American producers and workers must literally meet world-class standards. To help meet these challenges, developers and educators need to understand the nature of the global economy as well as the technologies shaping that economy.

Emergence of the Information Economy

Historically, communications improvements have profoundly altered the scope and nature of market activities. In the nonelectronic age, information moved slowly; markets were segmented and small; and distance was a major factor limiting economic growth. In the electronic age, information moves at the speed of light; markets are integrated and global; and the "concept of distance has finally lost its meaning" (Hogrebe, 1980, p. 1). In the most recent phase of the electronic age, digital telecommunications have revolutionized not only the speed and geographic scope of economic transactions but the very nature of the economic system.

This most recent phase coincides with the emergence of what has been called the information economy. In the information economy, the collection, storage, manipulation, analysis, and transmission of data are primary activities. Agricultural and manufacturing activities employ fewer and fewer workers while the information and service sectors employ more and more. Shifts in the composition of the national workforce mirror these changes. Today about 4 percent of the national workforce is employed in agriculture, 23 percent in manufacturing, and 73 percent in services. In ten years, 2 percent are projected to work in agriculture, 5 percent in manufacturing, and 93 percent in services (Crupi, 1989).

The transition to the information age has accelerated sharply in the last three decades. With the 1959 introduction of the chip—an integrated electronic circuit fabricated on a fleck of silicon—the ability to collect, store, manipulate, and analyze data made a quantum jump forward. Today a chip the size of a newborn's thumbnail can hold a million electronic components and perform a million calculations a second while drawing the same power as a nightlight. "The chip would be extraordinary enough if it were only low-cost electronics, but its ability to embody logic and memory also gives it the essence of human intellect. So, like the mind, the chip has virtually infinite application—and much the same potential to alter life fundamentally" (Boraiko, 1982, p. 421).

The revolution in microelectronics has been accompanied by equally portentous changes in telecommunications technology. The first commercial communications satellite was launched in 1965. This satellite made available 240 telephone circuits between the United States and Europe. The capacity required for these circuits could be used to provide one television circuit as well. "This one satellite, with only one television circuit, revolutionized communications across the Atlantic Ocean" (Rubin, 1983, p. 4).

But the revolution only began in 1965. In the years since, the number of satellite television circuits has increased more than tenfold and the number of telephone circuits has increased more than a hundredfold. Audio and visual communications now instantaneously link more than 146 countries around the world. Alvin Toffler's electronic global village is very nearly a reality.

Whereas satellites have stretched the geographic limits of communication, advances in fiber optics have greatly enhanced the efficiency of data transmissions. With potentially ten thousand times as much information capacity as copper circuits, fiber optic cables offer the prospect of ending communications congestion and fundamentally altering the information economy. The stage may be set "for an enrichment of life like that following the invention of the steam engine, the light bulb, and the transistor" (Kao, 1979, p. 516).

The technological advances in microelectronics and telecommunications are currently merging into what might be called the digital revolution. "In this phase, all the traditionally distinct media used for information transfer (such as telex), information storage (such as paper), and information processing (such as the human brain) converge into one medium: the computer network. The one carrier for all types of information will be the digital signal" (Hameling, 1983, p. 2). The ability to participate in the digital revolution will be essential for future local development.

Evolution of the Global Economy

The digital revolution and transportation improvements have made global financial and product markets possible. As a result, many local economies face intense international competition for customers and capital. The Department of Commerce estimates that the United States exports about one-fifth of its industrial production and that about 70 percent of all U.S. goods compete directly with foreign goods (President's Commission on Industrial Competitiveness, 1985).

The rapid transition to global markets has spawned new economic power centers and consolidated some old ones. The ranks of the top twenty exporting countries now include newly industrializing countries such as Korea, Taiwan, Hong Kong, Singapore, China, Mexico, and Brazil. The Pacific Rim countries currently account for a higher share of world exports than do the countries of Western Europe ("Trade Winds . . .," 1986). At the same time, Europe and the United States have tried to consolidate their positions with the European Economic Community and the North American Free Trade Agreement—alliances that embrace entire continents.

Participation in this evolving international economic order depends increasingly on the ability to use the new information technologies—computers and telecommunications. This is true, in part, because our major international competitors are themselves information economies. The information sector contributes more to gross domestic product in Canada, Japan, and several Western European countries than the combined agricultural and industrial sectors. This is also the case in many newly industrializing countries (Hameling, 1983).

Although information, broadly defined, is the most important good traded in world markets, the diversity of information services and physical commodities produced by the global economy is truly astonishing. In product lines ranging from computer software to automobiles, growing consumer demands for differentiated products have led firms to market niches and production processes requiring increasingly specialized workers and machines. Such unprecedented specialization, however, has increased the market volatility and financial risk faced by many firms.

As a result of these changes in the economic environment, diversification is no longer the strategy of choice; building defensible positions is. "In manufacturing industries this has meant using new technologies. The intensified use of automation equipment (numerically controlled machine tools, robotics, flexible manufacturing systems) constitutes part of the firms' strategy to improve production flexibility. The second major component of the firms' strategy in this area is to form networks of specialized suppliers. This suggests that the observed changes may lead to a new form of industrial organization—networks of small plants or firms clustered around particular large enterprises" (Acs, 1992, p. 43).

The new forms of business organization evolving from the digital revolution and the global information economy present economic development and continuing education specialists with unprecedented challenges—and opportunities.

Opportunities for Economic Developers

Economies develop when productivity and real per capita incomes grow over time. By definition, productivity increases when any innovation, either managerial or technical, increases output for a given cost or equivalently reduces the cost of producing a given output. An advanced telecommunications system can facilitate such cost-minimizing innovations and in the process increase competitiveness, generate new jobs, attract new businesses, and speed rural development.

Advanced telecommunications can increase competitiveness by lowering distribution, inventory, labor, scheduling, and managerial costs. Instantaneous communications often increase the efficiency of distribution systems, not only in dispatching but in monitoring expenses like freight handling, transport contractors' charges, and marketing costs. Inventory costs can be lowered by telecommunications-based ordering systems that detect shortages sooner and allow quicker, more frequent reorders. Labor savings may be realized by substituting telecommunications for the services of messengers, drivers, even guards. Scheduling costs can be reduced by the rapid communication of mechanical breakdowns, parts shortages, raw materials deficiencies, or other reasons for production stoppages. And managerial productivity can be increased if telecommunications-provided data result in better-informed administrative decisions (Jonscher, 1985).

Managerial productivity can also be enhanced by increased use of teleconferencing. According to one study, key company officials spend almost half their time in face-to-face meetings, with travel time to and from averaging three hours per meeting. "Much of this travel time is wasted: company time when the executive is out of touch and not productive. Worse, rough trips, frantic airport hopping, jet lag, and meals on the run all take a mental and physical toll on the traveler, further degrading effectiveness even when the executive or sales representative is on the job" (Singleton, 1983, p. 180). Teleconferencing also reduces travel costs. A Delaware chemical firm reports that in 1982 teleconferencing eliminated three hundred sixty-two trips and four thousand hours of employee travel time for a total savings of $500,000. The company claims that teleconferencing will eventually reduce its annual travel budget from $18 million to $10 million a year (Leddick, 1983).

A state-of-the-art telecommunications system also helps in the formation of job-creating small businesses. "One of the more innovative uses of telecommunications for small businesses is the expansion of their markets through telemarketing. Such usage is popular in Nebraska. In fact, Omaha has been called the '800 Capital of the World.' Omaha and the surrounding area are populated by telemarketing businesses that are intensive users of 800 and WATS services. These businesses employ a large number of Omaha's work force" (Williams, 1989, p. 57).

More generally, a sophisticated electronic infrastructure makes an area more attractive to all sorts of businesses. In a recent survey of corporate executives, 68 percent of the respondents indicated that the availability of telecommunications services was an "important" or "very important" consideration in their site selection decisions (Bergeron, 1988). Increasingly, industrial park evaluations include telecommunications capabilities as selection criteria. For many firms, the availability of fiber optic cable is especially important.

General Telephone Company of California (GTE), for example, runs a fiber optic cable directly into the communications building of the industrial park. One of the chief benefits is that installation time for new park tenants is reduced substantially. Whereas it may take a year in other locations to hook up to the telecommunications system, the hookup is completed in less than a month at parks already configured with fiber optic cable (Henry, 1988).

In addition, more and more firms are constructing office facilities with built-in communications networks. In the future, "companies building their own facilities will plan for such information outlets in the way they now plan for telephone outlets. Smaller businesses that rent office space will come to expect built-in communication networks that can be shared by tenants in the same way they now demand phone lines or air conditioning" (Singleton, 1983, p. 176).

The advantages of a sophisticated telecommunications network may be especially important for economic development of rural areas. A director of the National Association of Towns and Townships may well be correct in observing that "rural America is an opportunity we can't afford to pass up. Small communities can provide attractive, viable alternatives to the urban lifestyle, because the old objection that there are no jobs in rural America has a new answer. That answer lies with our emerging technologies. With computers and telecommunications links, many of America's jobs can be done anywhere. It is beginning to happen" (Cole, 1989, p. 90).

A modern telecommunications infrastructure, especially a telephone system with digital switching capabilities, could contribute significantly to narrowing urban-rural economic gaps. With information moving at the speed of light, geographic location is no longer a central consideration. Telecommunications-based increases in competitiveness, employment growth, and new business formations need not be confined to city dwellers. But how, specifically, will advanced telecommunications help rural areas?

First, better telecommunications can give farmers better information about prices, contract opportunities, and export markets. The cattle industry offers a good illustration of the importance of the instantaneous availability of accurate price information. "The new trend in many livestock-raising areas is direct buying; the buyer visits larger farms (minimum one thousand head of cattle), quotes a price, and makes the buy on the spot. Smaller farmers still have to take their cattle to market and that puts them at a serious disadvantage. If they think the price quoted upon arrival is too low, they do not have any feasible alternatives; maintaining the cattle at market or returning home are both too costly. So they end up being forced to take whatever price is offered" (Parker, Hudson, Dillman, and Roscoe, 1989, p. 141). With an advanced telecommunications system, the ranchers could telemarket their cattle all over the country (indeed all over the world) before physically transporting them to the buyers. Not surprisingly, however, the major meat packers have resisted cattle telemarketing experiments.

Second, the electronic infrastructure can help rural areas attract major corporations that are using enhanced telecommunications to relocate and decentralize operations. This trend is called *outsourcing,* a process by which major companies farm out certain basic production tasks to rural towns with cheap labor and rent (Parker, Hudson, Dillman, and Roscoe, 1989). General Motors Corporation, for example, has been able to successfully outsource to a huge production plant in Juarez, Mexico, by using telecommunications-intensive, computer-aided design and computer-aided manufacturing technologies. Given access to the information superhighway, many rural areas can be similarly attractive to outsourcing firms.

Finally, state-of-the-art telecommunications offer rural businesses the opportunity to export their services far beyond local markets. Increasingly, the production of traded goods and services depends on the efficiency and quality of such services as accounting, banking, legal services, and printing and design—services that can be exported via telecommunications. Currently, however, most rural-area business services are concentrated in activities with little export potential—wholesale and retail trade, other private services, and government. Thus, "the expansion of new and existing telecommunications technologies into rural area holds the promise of enabling the rural services sector to attract and foster the higher end services and information processing jobs on an equal footing with the urban areas" (Aspen Institute, 1989, p. 3).

In the information-based global economy, advanced telecommunications systems clearly offer local developers tremendous opportunities. Large opportunities, however, are usually accompanied by large challenges.

Challenges for Economic Developers

A central challenge to economic developers is the identification and procurement of electronic infrastructures that match the requirements of modern firms. An information-based economy requires sophisticated telecommunication systems as well as the traditional water, sewer, electric power, and transportation infrastructures. But what, specifically, are electronic infrastructures?

Clearly, a central part of the telecommunications infrastructure is the public telephone network, including local exchange carriers such as the Bell operating companies as well as long-distance and interexchange carriers like AT&T, MCI, and U.S. Sprint. From a development perspective, however, the telecommunications infrastructure cannot be defined so narrowly. A wide range of other telecommunications systems, such as value-added networks, cellular radio systems, paging networks, shared tenant services, metropolitan area networks, teleports, and cable television, can be used to meet the requirements of modern firms.

In addition, the telecommunications infrastructure can include so-called private networks—that is, telecommunications facilities used by a single firm or a closed group of firms. "For certain applications, such private networks can promote efficiency by permitting large users to develop customized solutions to their particular telecommunications needs and to employ telecommunications strategically to gain a competitive advantage in the marketplace" (U.S. Department of Commerce, 1990, p. 10). Given the variety and complexity of modern telecommunications systems, a key challenge to economic developers is the matching of local firm requirements with existing information technologies.

Once the appropriate electronic infrastructure has been identified, the next question is, How can economic developers help to procure such a telecommunications system? Answers can be found at the state, local, and industry levels.

To date, state public utility regulators and legislatures generally have been the focus of activities related to telecommunications and economic development. The most common state initiatives have been to provide regulatory flexibility and deregulation for telecommunications service providers. The New Jersey legislature, for example, passed a Telecommunications Act in 1992 that deregulated competitive telecommunications services and provided for other reforms aimed at streamlining the regulatory process. By the end of 1993, New Jersey Bell had installed about five hundred thousand miles of fiber optic cable throughout the state; the accelerated investment had resulted in advance service applications and trials including distance learning and telecommuting. A 1994 report of the New Jersey Board of Regulatory Commissioners looked "at real world examples of job development through either new firms moving into the state or existing companies electing to stay. What was found was very encouraging. The network deployment is less than one year old and already the benefits are there" (Southwestern Bell, 1994, p. 3). Although specific state policies will vary with individual circumstances, local developers should generally push for flexible policies that reduce regulatory delays and spur competition among telecommunications providers.

Urban area developers may want to consider narrower policies such as tax breaks and real estate concessions to lure telecommunications firms to their cities. The telecommunications firms, in turn, may prevent a business exodus from metropolitan high rents, taxes, and wages. The Port Authority of New York and New Jersey, for example, initiated the Teleport project in 1983 to keep banking, law, insurance, real estate, and other service firms from fleeing the Big Apple's high costs of doing business. At its inauguration, Teleport was expected to create more than five thousand jobs and generate more than $10 million in revenues for the surrounding localities (U.S. Department of Commerce, 1990).

At the industry level, most Bell operating companies and many independent local exchange carriers have economic development programs. Illinois Bell's strategy for economic development, for example, is to establish regional organizations to assist communities in attracting and retaining businesses (perhaps reasoning that business development also increases telecommunications usage and revenues) (U.S. Department of Commerce, 1990). Southwestern Bell sponsors development grants for Oklahoma communities with the best proposals for an Information Age Telecommunications Center and funds new computer labs, new business administration buildings, and new master's telecommunications programs at Oklahoma universities (Southwestern Bell, 1994). A general implication of these privately funded programs is that development professionals need to establish and maintain close working relationships with their local phone companies. The challenge is to cultivate such relationships while urging state officials to increase the competition faced by telecommunications firms.

To meet these challenges, economic developers need technical expertise, political acumen, and strong interpersonal skills. As the following case study shows, however, successful procurement of the right telecommunications infrastructure can yield substantial benefits to the local economy.

Case study: Pauls Valley and Southwestern Bell. Located about fifty miles south of Oklahoma City, Pauls Valley has a population of approximately six thousand people. In 1993, the national headquarters of a major local employer began to significantly increase voice and data communications with its local offices. Company executives told city officials that the Pauls Valley plant would be forced to relocate unless better telecommunications services could be obtained. Specifically, the local telephone system needed to be upgraded with digital switches to accommodate the firm's communications traffic.

After careful analysis, Southwestern Bell determined that the Pauls Valley digital switch investment would not be profitable. Rather than seeking an Oklahoma Corporation Commission order mandating the digital upgrade, city officials appointed a steering committee to seek the new switches. In committee chair Bill Humphrey's words, "rather than take an adversarial course, we sat down at the table and everyone arose a winner."

In December 1994, the Pauls Valley Industrial Authority and Southwestern Bell signed an innovative agreement. The industrial authority agreed to serve at least one year as an agent of Southwestern Bell and to sell enough telephone services to justify the switch investment. Southwestern Bell agreed to train selected city employees to sell specialized phone services like caller ID, call waiting, call forwarding, call trace, and others. If city agent sales generated annual revenues of at least $65,000, Southwestern Bell agreed to undertake the $1.2 million digital switch upgrade.

The agreement was a success. Pauls Valley is now equipped with digital switches. The major employer did not relocate, and local leaders now tout Pauls Valley as a "pretty little town" with a state-of-the-art electronic infrastructure.

Opportunities for Educators

Telecommunications holds great promise for improving access to education. Teleconferencing can provide distance learning to any suitably equipped location. By combining a critical mass of students with specialized instructors, interactive video broadcasts can improve the variety and quality of courses offered by rural high schools. And, unlike school district consolidations that move students physically to teachers, televised courses move teachers electronically to students (Parker, Hudson, Dillman, and Roscoe, 1989).

As an example, rural education research centers sponsored by the National Rural Education Association (NREA), one of which is located at the University of Oklahoma, serve rural school administrators, teachers, and students. The university's center currently provides satellite-delivered professional development programs for administrators and educators within the state's seventy-seven counties and holds videotape licensing agreements for these programs with rural school districts in ten other states. These distance education programs provide access to advanced education and training otherwise not available for rural educators. Using a variety of advanced technologies, the center also conducts electronic field trips for rural students by exposing young adults to content experts and practitioners of multiple professions. Students learn more about the subject matter and are able to evaluate career opportunities in fields representing the arts, humanities, and physical and social sciences.

Educational networks can also be extended to the business community as companies develop interactive training centers linked to public and private institutions. Currently, such U.S. corporations as AT&T, Digital Equipment, General Electric, Hewlett Packard, IBM, Motorola, NCR, and Xerox participate in the National Technological University (NTU), a satellite-based consortium of twenty-eight engineering universities. "NTU awards accredited master's degrees in engineering and material sciences as well as noncredit courses and workshops on advanced technology to 220 corporate and government research sites nationally. NTU is ranked among the top-quality postgraduate engineering institutions in the United States" (U.S. Department of Commerce, 1990, p. 30). Other educational networks designed to serve the business community include Colorado State University's SURGE program, which delivers graduate education in business, engineering, and computer science to working professionals. On-campus courses taught by university faculty are videotaped and then distributed to students along with supplemental course materials. The Virtual College teleprogram, administered by New York University and developed through support from the Alfred P. Sloan Foundation, is an on-line graduate teleprogram that trains professionals and managers. Using the Lotus Notes groupware package, students can complete the course from their home or office computers, collaborate over national data networks, and build business applications for their own organizations. The teleprogram delivers the same level of instruction that characterizes on-campus lectures, seminars, and laboratories. Course offerings use advanced technologies such as interactive video, virtual reality, hypertext libraries, and on-line laboratories (Peterson's Guides, 1993, p. 56).

A more localized application can be illustrated through the University of Oklahoma's delivery of graduate-level engineering programs to one of the state's major energy firms, Halliburton Services, through a compressed two-way video, two-way audio network. Students on the university campus receive simultaneous instruction with Halliburton employees located more than ninety miles from the campus in fully equipped compressed video classrooms. Halliburton employees can directly access advanced degrees without leaving the work site. In essence, continuing education centers can televise interactive seminars for doctors, lawyers, accountants, bankers, nurses, architects, air traffic controllers, economic developers—any group of workers needing professional updating or periodic retraining.

Telecommunications can expand educational opportunities well beyond secondary schools, business firms, and professional groups, however. With the proper infrastructure, homemakers can learn Japanese or astrophysics in their dens. Junior and senior citizens can browse electronically through the best libraries in the world while researchers swap data files, exchange technical drawings, even talk with their colleagues. Using telecommunications, the potential for more people to acquire more education is simply immense. Unfortunately, the obstacles to electronic education are also large.

Challenges for Educators

Many educators fail to use the information technologies in ways that truly enhance education. "Either there is no interaction between students and teachers, the video is 'boring talking heads,' or 'glitzy production values get in the way of education'" (Parker, Hudson, Dillman, and Roscoe, 1989, p. 146). If lectures are broadcast in sixty-minute segments (with no commercial breaks or music), for example, student torpor may be as immense as the potential of distance learning.

In addition, many of the people who most need to be reached—for basic literacy and skills training, for example—are not in institutional settings such as schools and workplaces (Parker, Hudson, Dillman, and Roscoe, 1989). To be effective, of course, the new technologies must be used. But the new electronic devices are daunting enough for educated urbanites; the comfort level with these machines is no doubt lower among the uneducated and those living in rural areas. A major challenge to electronic education is to devise settings in which the illiterate and unskilled feel comfortable enough to experiment with the new technologies.

Despite these limitations and obstacles, electronic information flows can significantly improve education. Equipped with computers, digital switches, fiber optic cables, and communication satellites, learning institutions throughout the country can become educational models in the information age. Less grandly, if educators do not acquire these capabilities, their competitive positions will erode and eventually become untenable.

Conclusion

The digital revolution and the information economy are realities that will grow more important in the coming decades. Already the information industry grows faster and employs more people than any other. The national and international economic systems are crucially and increasingly dependent on instantaneous communications. There is little evidence that these trends will be reversed; indeed, they are likely to accelerate.

If these observations are correct, an advanced telecommunications network is essential for future economic growth. The central feature of every information-based economy is the ability to move electronic zeroes and ones over long distances at fantastic speeds. Computers and telecommunications are as essential for information capitalism as raw materials and railroads were to industrial capitalism. A twentieth-century state without an advanced telecommunications system would be as competitively disadvantaged as a late-nineteenth-century state without a railroad.

Advanced telecommunications can help firms expand markets, reduce costs, and create jobs; attract new companies and diversify a local economy; reduce the urban-rural economic gap; and help firms become more globally competitive and make an area more attractive to international investors. In these ways and others, advanced telecommunications can set the stage for an enrichment of life as revolutionary as that following the steam engine, the light bulb, and the transistor. The challenge to economic development and education specialists is to make that enrichment possible.

References

Acs, Z. J. "Small Business Economics: A Global Perspective." *Challenge*, Nov./Dec. 1992, pp. 38–44.

Aspen Institute for Humanistic Studies. "Rural America in the Information Age." News release, May 1989, pp. 1–3.

Bergeron, T. "Corporate Executives Rate Site Selection Factors." *Area Development*, Dec. 1988, pp. 29–33.

Boraiko, A. A. "The Chip." *National Geographic*, 1982, *164* (4), 421–456.

Cole, A. "Telecommunications Can Bring Back the Vitality to Rural America." *Governing*, May 1989, pp. 90–94.

Crupi, J. A. "Regional Community Leadership in the 1990s." Speech given at the National Association of Regional Councils, Houston, Tex., May 1989.

Hameling, C. J. *Finance and Information: A Study of Converging Interests*. Norwood, N.J.: ABLEX, 1983.

Henry, D. L. "Telecommunications Services." *Area Development*, July 1988, pp. 108–112.

Hogrebe, F. M. (ed.). "Dangers and Opportunities of Digital Communication Media." Report prepared for ILET, Mexico City, April 1980.

Jonscher, C. "Assessing the Benefits of Telecommunications." *Intermedia*, Jan. 1985, pp. 21–24.

Kao, C. K., quoted in Boraiko, A. A. "Harnessing Light by a Thread." *National Geographic*, 1979, *156* (4), 516–535.

Leddick, K. "Hotels Hosting Increasing Number of Large Multi-City Teleconferences." *Communications News*, Feb. 1983, pp. 65–69.

Parker, E., Hudson, H., Dillman, D., and Roscoe, A. *Rural America in the Information Age: Telecommunications Policy for Rural Development*. Latham, Md.: University Press of America, 1989.

Peterson's Guides. National University Continuing Education Association (NUCEA). *The Electronic University: A Guide to Distance Learning*. Princeton, N.J.: National University Continuing Education Association, 1993.

President's Commission on Industrial Competitiveness. *Global Competition: The New Reality*. Washington, D.C.: President's Commission on Industrial Competitiveness, 1985.

Rubin, M. R. *Information Economics and Policy in the United States*. Littleton, Colo.: Libraries Unlimited, 1983.

Singleton, L. A. *Telecommunications in the Information Age*. Cambridge, Mass.: Ballinger, 1983.

Southwestern Bell Telephone Company. "Telecommunications: Advantage Oklahoma." Spring 1994, *2* (1), 1–5.

"Trade Winds Blowing Across the Pacific." *The Economist*, May 3, 1986, p. 89.

Williams, F. *The Competitive Challenge: Interchange Carriers and State Telecommunications Policy*. Austin, Tex.: Center for Research on Communication Technology and Society, 1959.

U.S. Department of Commerce. *Comprehensive Study of the Domestic Telecommunications Infrastructure*. National Telecommunications Infrastructure. National Telecommunications Information Administration. Jan. 1990.

WILL CLARK is associate professor of economics at the University of Oklahoma.

Community development offers unique opportunities for collaboration with communities and enhanced opportunities for their residents.

Maximizing Community Development Through Collaboration

Russell Usnick, Chris Shove, Francine Gissy

The term *community development* lacks a universally accepted single definition and also has several distinct term-of-art meanings when used in different contexts. *Community* itself is a value-laden term that generates many definitions (Galbraith, 1990). In the broadest usage, *community development* encompasses a wide array of community improvement activities that can range from informal neighborhood improvement meetings to vast, formal capital improvement schemes. As noted by the Community Development Society, "community is complex and multidimensional" and "the human dimension, which is capable of growth and development, is the most critical aspect of community" (Community Development Society, 1995). The Society believes that "the development of each community can be fostered through improved individual, organizational, and problem-solving skills" (Community Development Society, 1995).

Community development can indicate a communitywide, integrated, professional community-improvement activity that includes an economic development component. Many communities put all development activities, including economic development, under a department of community development. But community development can also describe a small-scale, single-purpose, grass-roots activity that might be the first germination of some future economic development activity. For both economic and community development, building community coalitions to create an appropriate vision for the community is an important role (Desai and Margenthaler, 1994).

Large-scale, formal community development programs are usually found in urban settings. In smaller cities, fewer of the community development functions are professionally staffed, and in many rural communities, there is no formal structure for addressing such issues. In one sense, informal community devel-

 NEW DIRECTIONS FOR HIGHER EDUCATION, no. 97, Spring 1997 © Jossey-Bass Publishers

opment activities occur in all communities. In rural settings where there is no formal community development structure, informal activities comprise the entirety of such activities. In urban settings, informal, nonprofessional activities exist and interface with the formal, professional community development infrastructure. For example, an ad hoc committee to improve the appearance of a small commercial area might work with a community development professional.

A wide range of persons engage in community development activities, both urban and rural. Economic development professionals work in many capacities in community development. Economic development professionals may do detailed economic modeling for one area but in another may meet with businesses to develop complex area plans. Community development specialists provide targeted services that can be highly technical or very general. Technical support might take the form of detailed analyses of building conditions or employment patterns, whereas general activities may simply include community organizing. Community leaders, both elected and volunteer, are continually involved in community development activities. Many types of community activists are key players in community development. Within the university, there are a number of actual and potential participants in community development. These individuals can include university leadership, faculty, administrative staff, research or extension associates, and students.

University as Partner in Community Development

Universities and colleges can be a significant resource for community economic development if they are properly used. Furthermore, due to a tightening of university budgets, increased scrutiny by legislators and citizens, and concomittant demands for more community service, universities are more willing to become active partners in community development activities. Universities want to demonstrate a responsiveness to their regions, and active collaboration with communities is an excellent approach. However, universities have a corporate culture that must be understood by those who wish to access their institutional services.

Generally, the missions of the university are to engage in teaching, research, and service—each with its own subtleties. *Teaching* includes not only traditional classroom instruction but also continuing education programs for career advancement, cultural enhancement, or perhaps distance learning programs. Real-world experience in the form of laboratory courses or internships is a growing component of many curriculums. The *research* mission of the university is to expand and disseminate knowledge. A faculty member is expected to actively add to the knowledge base in his or her discipline. In addition, the faculty member is expected to disseminate the results of the research so that it is available to others. Research is often driven by client or agency funding, but in many cases, research is conducted primarily out of a faculty member's own interest and expertise in a particular topic. The *service* mission specifically addresses the relationship between the university and the community at large. Faculty members are expected to provide service to entities both inside and outside of the university. Such service can include membership on university committees or participation in a center or an institute within the university. It can also include service to a national or international organization. Community support is considered university service, and as such, serves the mission of the university as well as the obligation of the faculty member. Higher education's service mission and the service obligation for faculty members can be a valuable resource for community development. Community development activities can be incorporated into this mission of the university and potentially can be seen as important to a broadened view of faculty tenure and promotion activities.

Establishing University and Community Collaboration

If a community seeks economic development technical assistance from a university, there are several ways to proceed. Given the changing focus of the university toward increased community support, most institutions will offer at least one, if not several points of contact for inquiries or additional information. An initial approach is to request a list of faculty who instruct or conduct research in areas related to community development issues. This might include faculty in economics, social work, urban and regional planning, business, or geography, to name a few. If the university has a centralized office for economic development, this is also an excellent starting point. In general, communities should seek to identify a faculty member, department, or center with a specific interest in their issue for consultation.

Citing the university service mission is one way to leverage free or low-cost university services for community development assistance. Communities should realize that, although the service mission is important, it often does not weigh as heavily with respect to the missions of teaching and research. However, university service is often highly valued by state legislatures, and as budgetary pressures rise, the service mission of the university takes on additional importance.

The logistics of securing collaboration between the university and the community vary depending on the type of service assistance required and the delivery vehicle. The following sections of this chapter explore some of the potential programs and services available through universities and how to access them.

Collaboration Opportunities for Communities and Universities

Continuing higher education represents more than a technical intervener in community development. The possible roles for collaboration are extensive and are based on technical assistance or general applications. *Technical assistance* activities are designed to provide specific community development services to the community, whereas *general application* activities cover a wider range and may be more innovative and integrative in nature. These categories are by no means exclusive. Training, for instance, can provide specific technical knowledge or it can provide general information for community leaders that is critical to community and economic development.

Unlike technical assistance, general applications, which are often referred to as *collaboration for innovation*, have far less concrete goals and generally involve interfacing with diverse community development entities to organize, facilitate, inform, or educate. Writers have discussed at length the relationship between action and learning that occurs in communities (Knox, 1992, and Friedmann, 1987).

Conventional wisdom has long held that a major research university appears to be a necessary condition for local high-tech economic development, but alone it is not sufficient to guarantee economic development (Feldman, 1994). A collaboration for innovation may either be purposive and focused or accidental and unfocused.

Common Community Economic Development Outreach Programs

In most states, at least one university operates a center that is specifically established to provide community economic development technical assistance. However, in some states, several universities may operate multiple technical assistance centers. These university-based centers provide a milieu of services that can include business planning, market research, technical feasibility studies in manufacturing, community development planning, business operations, financial counseling and packaging, and referrals. The most common types of centers found at universities are described in the following paragraphs. Many of these centers are partially funded by the federal government.

Small business development centers (SBDCs). Small business development centers are funded by the U.S. government's Small Business Administration. SBDCs have the mission of providing business technical assistance to small businesses in their university's region. SBDCs are noted for having a wealth of free information provided by the federal government and offer hundreds of instructional brochures for almost every business topic. SBDC staff normally are prepared to organize workshops on various business topics for communities within their region as well as one-to-one counseling with business operators on topics such as finance and business planning. The SBDC is an excellent place to find out about federal loan guarantee programs that help to leverage private bank loans.

In some SBDCs, there is sufficient staff to provide in-depth technical assistance such as researching and writing a business plan that will be used to acquire funding. For example, a Florida SBDC assisted a female entrepreneur by researching the market for a new type of clothing accessory. The SBDC team contacted numerous large retailers to assess their interest in the accessory and to determine how to introduce new clothes to large department store buyers. This information, along with cost and management information, were compiled into a formal business plan. The SBDC team advised the entrepreneur to find corporate joint-venture capital and aided in identifying possible candidates. With the SBDC plan, the entrepreneur was able to secure over $40,000 from a clothing manufacturing firm looking for a new product line. The entrepreneur and the firm produced and packaged the accessories and convinced one of the largest retailers to test the product in its Chicago stores.

U.S. Economic Development Administration (EDA) university centers. Economic Development Administration university centers are located in almost every state and provide technical assistance for community economic development statewide. The specific activities of the EDA centers may vary, but most centers conduct economic development studies, community business plans, and workshops and often employ interns to assist with community economic development projects. Most EDA centers require fees to cover costs. EDA centers are most highly recognized for carrying out detailed community economic development studies or plans. To locate the EDA university center in a given state, it is best to contact the state's U.S. Economic Development Administration representative, who is normally based in the capital city. Federal agency representatives are typically listed with government offices in the telephone directory.

A representative example of EDA center community development technical assistance is the provision of trained graduate student interns to needy communities. The university center hires graduate students from regional and city planning, economics, business, geography, and other disciplines and mentors them through an intensive economic development training program. The center simultaneously contacts communities that need assistance, thus evaluating the students and the potential community projects for a logical fit of talent and need. Students are then assigned to matching communities to work on a specific project for the summer. The center pays the intern's salary, and the community provides free housing and an office. The outcomes of these internships have resulted in large grants to build industrial parks, small business incubators, and downtown improvements or to establish revolving loan pools for entrepreneurs. In some cases, an intern's work on a target industry project has resulted in the siting of new industries in a particular community.

The University of Oklahoma's EDA University Center has operated an intern program for the past three years. Graduate students from business, public administration, regional and city planning, and engineering have participated in the summer intern program. Example projects include developing a conceptual plan for a lakeside city park and recreation area; designing an economic impact study for a proposed bacon packaging plant in the rural town of Thomas, Oklahoma; and completing a comprehensive assessment of tourism potential for a city recovering from the state's economic downturn of the 1980s.

National Aeronautics and Space Administration (NASA) technical assistance centers. NASA technical assistance centers are located in most states, with some centers providing services to multiple states. The NASA centers are focused on the transfer of NASA aviation and space technology to commercial users. In some cases a community may have an existing firm or start-up business that could benefit from a NASA technology. For example, the centers can query their extensive databases to identify technologies that may be exploited by a firm for a commercial application.

U.S. Department of Agriculture (USDA) Extension Services. USDA university extension services are located in every state and can be very helpful in community economic development, especially for rural areas. USDA university extension services can provide direct technical assistance in agricultural issues, and many such centers are also capable in business planning, economic development studies, and financial packaging plans. A state's Department of Agriculture can assist communities in identifying the nearest USDA university extension service center.

University Community Development Resources

Besides formally established university-based technical assistance centers, there are numerous, more informal resources that can be used for community economic development. Some of these resources are described in the following paragraphs.

Student technical assistance. Graduate students with expertise in a particular subject area are often an excellent yet cost-effective technical assistance resource. Almost all graduate students are required to conduct a research project to fulfill degree requirements. Consequently, they may be very interested in working on a community economic development project that can be incorporated into an academic project. Departments of urban planning, landscape architecture, social work, geography (economic), public administration, and economics are most likely to know of interested students. Many students seek long-term internship opportunities, allowing communities to access their technical assistance throughout a semester or for multiple years. Students generally require compensation due to the availability of numerous paid intern opportunities. However, it is likely communities can obtain a reduced rate from that normally charged by a professor or practicing professional in the field.

A notable example of student assistance having a statewide effect can be illustrated with a graduate thesis. In the authors' state, there has been a continuing concern about the lack of venture-capital financing for start-up and expanding businesses. Based on this concern, a student surveyed all venture-capital firms in the United States to identify those willing to invest in Oklahoma businesses and the types of investment interests. The student's national survey was very successful, receiving hundreds of responses from credible venture-capital firms. The information was compiled into a resource book for economic development organizations throughout the state. These organizations then distributed the book to entrepreneurs to develop start-up or expanded business across the state.

Class-based technical assistance. Class projects are an excellent way to acquire low-cost technical expertise. Generally, a group of students will work under the direction of a professor with extensive expertise in the subject area. For community economic development, the best types of academic departments to contact for class technical assistance are urban and regional planning, landscape architecture, social work (specializing in community development), geography (economic), public administration, and economics. Graduate-level studio or laboratory courses are particularly well suited for these projects because they meet more often with the objective of conducting an applicable project. A potential disadvantage of this approach, however, is that the students and professor also are trying to accomplish academic objectives that may not be focused entirely on a community's specific needs.

An example of class-based technical assistance is depicted through a collaborative project between an institution's regional and city planning and landscape architecture departments and a local community to develop long-range development plans for the surrounding city. To determine the project's scope, faculty met with city staff and selected objectives that could be accomplished by the students in the given time period. Over a one-year period, the studios conducted two distinct analyses. The first was a citywide environmental analysis to identify areas most and least suitable for development. In the second analysis, the students conducted a detailed review of economic, demographic, land use, political, and transportation issues to identify significant trends. These analyses resulted in three alternative district development plans that were later used by the community to identify potential economic development scenarios.

University department research service agreements. Another innovative way to acquire technical assistance is to establish a research service contract with a university department. Basically, a research service contract entails the provision of a graduate student to work on a project as a paid intern under the direct supervision of a faculty member. Besides intern compensation, additional funds should be expected for project expenses and a modest overhead payment. In this model, communities can receive low-cost technical assistance, which is particularly effective for projects that can be conducted on the university campus. As an example, a university department established a one-year research service contract with several local governments for graduate students to input city maps and city information into a computer geographic information system. This arrangement eliminated the need for cities to buy unique and expensive computer equipment and did not require hiring new or diverting existing city staff to complete this one-time project.

Specialized University Community Development Resources

Almost all universities and faculty are interested in conducting sponsored research or educational projects. The designation research project should not deter a community from using this approach. To the contrary, many universities and faculty have the capabilities and are keenly interested in practical or applied research rather than basic or curiosity research. In addition, many universities want to deliver education programs that are focused on practical needs of human or community development. As an example, a professor might conduct a lecture on economic development for the directors of a chamber of commerce. The professor provides the academic background on the subject and then leads the directors through an application-oriented exercise focused on individual needs. Another example is for a continuing education unit to sponsor several seminars for economic development professionals on how to use the new technologies of geographic information systems for economic development purposes. These technologies are regularly covered in several university courses, so it is easy to package them as short seminars.

Faculty research. For short-term (six months or less) projects, faculty research contracts are ideal. Although many faculty members may have the expertise needed for a community economic development project, their professional demands may not allow them to engage in long-term projects. With sufficient funds, however, the faculty members can be engaged for longer periods by buying their time out of teaching to devote it to research. The optimal time to employ faculty consultants for full-time research is usually during the summer when they have few or no teaching responsibilities. It is also important to recognize that because of the research mission, faculty are more likely to participate in community assistance projects that can also be utilized for academic publication.

Continuing education. In continuing education, most universities seek to establish programs that are self-supporting. Most have well-equipped meeting or conferencing facilities and available resources for community economic development activities. Whether it is for training chamber of commerce professionals in strategic planning or providing computer entry skills for a new business thinking of locating in a community, the university is prepared to accomplish the task. If the community can clearly identify a training need and some preferred instructors, the typical university continuing education unit can translate that idea into a training program with seminar fees to cover costs and possibly provide a profit to the community. Generally, if continuing education manages the entire training program, communities do not have to be concerned with facilities, logistics, training materials, or program budgeting. The university continuing education unit can provide all of these services. The best way to begin is to contact the university's continuing education program coordinator to discuss the seminar idea and the potential enrollment.

Special university research centers. Many universities, especially in major urban areas, have internally funded research and service centers that can be very helpful in community economic development projects. Many of these centers are specifically created to assist in societal problem solving. Although most centers require payment for their services, others perform work out of a sense of commitment to the communities in which they serve. Social science departments are most likely to house these types of centers. For example, the University of Oklahoma's Center for Applied Social Policy Studies conducts applied research activities tied with measuring and evaluating social change within communities. The center compiles demographic profiles and conducts needs assessments, program evaluations, and impact studies for organizations and communities. Often these types of research centers are not well known within the university; however, the president's office will likely maintain a directory of such resources.

Case Studies: Bringing It All Together

Two projects that occurred at the authors' institution aptly demonstrate the value of university and community collaboration. The first demonstrates the collaborative use of technical assistance for an international project, and the second demonstrates the application of collaboration for innovation on a more local level.

The first scenario begins with a faculty member's contact with a Russian economic institute. After describing the university's continuing education programs in economic development, the economic institute agreed to act as a partner for the university and identified Russian organizations that would be willing to attend the institution's economic development programs. It was agreed that costs to attend the programs would be shared by the university, the economic institute, and Russian participants. The university provided campus housing, the program sponsor agreed to waive the registration fees, the economic institute provided international logistics, and the Russian officials paid their own airfare. Based on this shared-cost partnership, two important factors occurred when the Russian officials arrived at the university: (1) because they paid for part of their training, they perceived themselves as equal partners in this international endeavor; and (2) this partnership then led them to describe other needs of their Russian cities. Revealing these needs resulted in additional collaborative opportunities. For example, a Russian power company official, the Russian economic institute, and a university faculty member jointly planned a project to provide research and assistance to develop a new town in a region of Russia. This region was experiencing a lack of housing and economically viable activities. As part of the cooperative plan, Russian officials agreed to provide free housing and meals for the researchers. The economic institute agreed to handle international logistics and to conduct the economic study for the plan. The faculty member agreed to perform the required research for little compensation and, in fact, received a grant from the university for airfare and graduate research assistants. Furthermore, the Russian power company agreed to engage the services of a Russian architectural institute to assist with technical details.

Two faculty members and two graduate students from the institution traveled to Russia, paying their airfare and receiving housing, meals, excursions, and some compensation for their work. Upon arrival, the economic institute arranged for housing, office space, and transportation to the work site. The team members completed their work over the summer, resulting in a published academic article and a life-changing experience for the students. The economic institute was subsequently invited to provide seminars on the Russian economy to U.S. oil executives, and the Russian power company used the research report to receive political support and funding to build the new town. In addition, while in northern Russia, the faculty member and graduate students were asked by yet another city to assist and train city staff on their development project. Today, the team still collaborates in World Bank-related projects.

This scenario illustrates the numerous possibilities for one initial, well-devised collaborative endeavor between a university and community—even at an international level. However, this type of collaboration doesn't just happen and in fact requires three primary elements to ensure a mutually beneficial result: (1) negotiating a win-win agreement by arranging for a significant role for each collaborator, (2) developing a relationship of trust and cooperation, and (3) as much as possible sharing the financial requirements to promote an equal partnership.

The second scenario begins with the development of a strategic plan for the Center for Business and Economic Development, part of the College of Continuing Education at the University of Oklahoma. As part of the planning process, a group of community development professionals, economic development professionals, civic leaders (state chamber representative, city manager), faculty, and business people from across the state served voluntarily on an advisory committee. During one of the meetings, a discussion evolved concerning the somewhat fragmented character of community development in the state. Although a great deal of community and economic development activity occurs across the state, the interaction between the various organizations seemed sporadic and uneven. Of particular concern was the often insufficient knowledge of the prominent service activities by those who could most benefit. Subsequent discussions led to the formation of a steering committee to establish a conference that would include as many diverse groups and interests related to community and economic development as possible. These discussions led to the first annual statewide community development conference, titled *Expanding Our Community Horizons* and held in June 1994.

The conference assembled twenty-five state and regional organizations to offer tools and techniques for those involved in community development. Both the public and private sectors as well as community volunteers were urged to attend. The goal of the conference was to pool the resources of all organizations involved in community development. Each year, many state organizations sponsor community development conferences at varying times and places. Although this diversity is good, it is a confusing process to determine which conferences to attend, expensive if attending multiple conferences, and difficult for financial sponsors who are solicited repeatedly throughout the year. The conference's new collaborative approach simplified the process by keeping costs down and reducing stakeholders' time attending several conferences.

The uniqueness of the conference stemmed from the fact that all management functions were conducted on a voluntary basis by the steering committee. These individuals were representatives of chambers of commerce, community and economic development organizations, the state department of commerce, utilities, universities, and convention and tourism offices. Also on the steering committee were city managers, bankers, and city and county officials. Subcommittees were formed to address the following areas: site location, topics, speakers, sponsorships, trade show development, and marketing brochures. Participants were identified by tapping database lists from the steering committee (such as other universities, the Municipal League, state chamber of commerce). The Oklahoma Department of Commerce used its internal resources to develop and print marketing materials, and the University of Oklahoma's University Center coordinated the registrations.

Presentations were made by community leaders and included case studies in seven areas—capacity building, community health care, finance, finance-infrastructure, economic development organizations, solid waste, and job creation. Breakout sessions focused on specific community development topics and were designed to provide practical examples of how a community problem was resolved. Tradeshow booths provided one-to-one contact for participants who wanted to obtain additional information.

The conference drew an attendance of nearly two hundred people and far exceeded expectations. Fund-raising, coupled with conference fees, generated a budget surplus. Sponsors included arts councils; electric cooperatives; incubator business associations; certified cities programs; chambers of commerce; the city managers association; the cooperative extension service; the state department of commerce, tourism and recreation; vocational-technology schools; a state Economic Development Council; utilities; business centers at two state universities; the state chamber of commerce; banks; and substate planning districts. Approximately twenty organizations participated, as sponsors and in the concurrent trade show.

A post-conference meeting was held to review and critique the community development conference, resulting in the following conclusions and recommendations for future conferences:

- From the outset it was recognized that marketing limitations were going to occur. It was suggested that it might be more beneficial to target groups of volunteers and chambers of commerce in communities along with state-elected representatives to market future conferences.
- Some of those scheduled to make presentations did not attend, although confirmation letters were sent to all presenters. The timing in organizing the event was questioned as to whether or not the responsibilities were delegated early enough for duties to be accomplished. Suggestions were made to have a moderator set up and confirm session events or to use sponsorship money to subcontract for a conference coordinator position.
- The overall conference was a success, with sessions targeting the needs of the audience. It was determined that future conferences of this nature should be held.

The university is by nature a place where diverse groups interface in many ways. The potential for innovative approaches in community development is significant when collaboration includes the university. The foregoing example is but one of hundreds of cases where community development issues are innovatively addressed through collaborative activities.

Adult and continuing education models offer strong potential for expanding a community's knowledge, skill base, and appreciation for community development issues. Activities can be scheduled in a community across several topics, or alternatively a single topic that occurs in a number of communities could be addressed. The variety of possible structural approaches offers great opportunity (Galbraith, 1990).

Conclusion

Successful community development is complex. An excellent scheme can fail due to interest rate shifts in the national market. A mediocre program can become a stunning success due to an unexpected plant or commercial area opening. It is often hard to replicate successful applications. An approach that is successful in a community at this time may fail miserably at a later date or in another community. It is sometimes hard to separate success and failure in community development. A seemingly failed community development effort may provide fertile seeds for the future. Even so, successful past projects are often the most reliable starting point in community development.

Both communities and adult and continuing education leaders should think in terms of developing ongoing programs, not just courses (Mulcrone, 1993). To the extent possible, the university should view itself as a consultant concerned with the entrepreneurial aspects of program development. Likewise, communities should seek to structure the collaboration so that it expands and enhances their capabilities and abilities. For example, technical assistance with a training component for local personnel who can continue the effort makes for much stronger community development programs. Training that leaves the capability of passing new knowledge to others expands the scope of community development and paves the way for others' involvement in the future. Community development is a continuous activity in every community. Making it functional and effective is vitally important to communities and to the people who live in them.

References

Community Development Society. "World Wide Web Home Page." [http://www.infoana-lytic.com/cds]. June 1995.

Desai, H., and Margenthaler, C. "Creating an Economic Development Strategy: Modeling A City/Development Organization/College Partnership." *Economic Development Review,* 1994, 12 (3), 37–41.

Feldman, M. "The University and Economic Development: The Case of Johns Hopkins University and Baltimore." *Economic Development Quarterly,* 1994, 8 (1), 67–76.

Friedmann, J. *Planning in the Public Domain.* Princeton, N.J.: Princeton University Press, 1987.

Galbraith, M. *The Nature of Community and Adult Education.* New Directions for Adult and Continuing Education, no. 47. San Francisco: Jossey-Bass, 1990.

Knox, A. *Comparative Perspectives on Professionals' Ways of Learning.* New Directions For Adult and Continuing Education, no. 55. San Francisco: Jossey-Bass, 1992.

Mulcrone, P. *Developing Internal and External Program Resources.* New Directions for Adult and Continuing Education, no. 60. San Francisco: Jossey-Bass, 1993.

RUSSELL USNICK is associate professor of regional and city planning at the University of Oklahoma.

CHRIS SHOVE is assistant professor of regional and city planning at the University of Oklahoma.

FRANCINE GISSY is director of the Center for Business and Economic Development in the College of Continuing Education at the University of Oklahoma.

*A global economy coupled with the advance of high technology has
produced a very different set of needs for community college involvement in local and regional economic development.*

Community Economic Development
Through Community Colleges

Jerry W. Young

The community college is a uniquely American innovation, one adapted to the
American form of democracy. In fact, at various times different writers have
referred to community colleges as "democracy's colleges," primarily because of
their open access. Kerr has called the community college one of America's "two
great innovations in higher education" (Deegan and Tillery, 1985, p. vii), the
other being the development of the land-grant college in the nineteenth century.

Deegan and Tillery (1985) have outlined the history of community colleges into five generations, the first four of which have already passed for many
community colleges. Succinctly, these generations are: (1) extension of high
school, 1900–1930; (2) junior college, 1930–1950; (3) community college,
1950–1970; (4) comprehensive community college, 1970–1985; (5) new college, 1985–present. One might argue with the name given to each generation,
the beginning and ending dates, or the fact that the vocational-technical function has been understated, but clearly the community colleges have been very
responsive educational institutions to societal change.

The fifth generation presents the greatest dilemma for analysis. One can
achieve a frame of reference with regard to the operating environments of community colleges in the present from documents such as the one published by
Macomb Community College. The document produced by Macomb's Institute
for Future Studies states that "community profiles are becoming more
diverse. . . . Since community colleges tend to mirror the communities they
serve, America's two-year institutions are becoming more dissimilar. . . . Quite
simply, what leads to progress on one campus may result in status quo—or
worse—at another. . . . The continuing common denominator is that all community colleges must remain community based and locally focused. The new

74

paradox is that the method and degree of response may be as diverse as the communities in which two-year institutions are located" (Macomb Community College, 1992, p. 1).

Deegan and Tillery suggest that the greatest single change with which community colleges have had to cope is the shift from internal to external control. This influence over institutional destiny is directed through state and federal laws and regulations, court precedents, public funding, and pressures from various self-interest groups, all of which control and influence community college operations. External issues have become so pronounced in the 1990s that the college chief executive officer must devote a large percentage of his or her time to them. Paradoxically, community colleges are most needed for local responsiveness to their unique communities, but they are increasingly controlled at the state level, which forces which toward uniformity.

Community Development

Community development is any activity or improvement that enhances the value and attractiveness of a community. Many now agree that economic development is a part of the much larger area of community development, and the larger purpose of economic development is the improvement and strengthening of communities. Mark Waterhouse, an attorney, community development professional, and consultant, outlines the relationship of economic development to community development and concludes that "the proper job for the economic developer today is not just a concern for business, jobs, taxes, and economics. Healthy, viable communities must be the ultimate goal, and all efforts must be focused in that direction" (Koepke, 1991, p. 12).

As Deegan and Tillery have pointed out, community colleges have had a focus on serving their local communities since 1950. Community services is often a separate administrative division found within community colleges, and most community colleges see such service as part of their mission. The American Association of Community Colleges (AACC) has an associate organization named ComBase (community-based organizations), which serves as an umbrella association for those seeking to improve the community development aspect of community colleges. Many of the community colleges that have strong economic development programs are members of ComBase.

Historically, education has been understood, from a social and cultural perspective, to be a part of community development. However, few have understood the role education plays in economic development. Traditionally, education has been inwardly focused, meaning that if people wanted to be educated or trained, they had to be admitted formally to an institution. The external focus of most educational institutions has often been limited to scholarship fund-raising, enrichment (for example, theater or concerts), athletics, or various types of continuing education that were primarily an extension of traditional curricula.

Community development comprises the economic, social, and cultural elements that give a geographical area its identity. The very depth and breadth of these elements further reflect and define each community. There is an obvious point of common purpose for economic development and community colleges in the broader goal of enhancing community development. It is in the community development context that government leaders, the business community, community colleges, the various public service providers, and economic development professionals can find common ground.

Economic Development

Defining economic development and the special terms that are a part of economic development presents a problem. For example, just within community colleges, terms such as employer-based training, customized training, contract education, business training, industrial training, technology training, pre-employment training, job training, technical training, and job retraining are related because they all involve training, but the emphasis is somewhat different for each use. The use and emphasis of these terms may shift from one part of the country to another.

New literature on economic development, as practiced by community colleges and national programs such as the Keeping America Working project, is beginning to create a common lexicon of terms. Most of the literature on the contribution and involvement of community colleges in economic development has been published since 1985. A literature review shows that the AACC has published much of the material focusing on the role of community colleges in economic development, primarily through the association's professional journal. Jossey-Bass and the American Society for Training and Development have published some important works on economic development, which are very useful to community colleges involved in economic development. Of particular value have been Anthony P. Carnevale's works, *The Learning Enterprise* (1989), *Quality Education for the New American Economy* (1994), and *Workplace Basics: The Essential Skills Employers Want* (1991). In addition, several theses by students attending the American Council on Economic Development's Economic Development Institute (EDI) have focused on community colleges' role in economic development. Examples include *The Role of the American Community College in Economic Development* (1993), *Community Education and the Relationship to Economic Development* (1991), and *The Effects of the Community College on Industrial Growth* (1983).

Economic development is as old as civilization, dating back to the time when humans began to alter the earth for some economic advantage. Yet, as a profession, economic development is very new. As the number and complexity of issues affecting economic development have increased, the need for agents to serve as brokers and managers of the process has also increased.

Both the newness of the economic development profession and the high rate of change affecting the profession have created a field with a diverse range of activities and no consensus regarding a definition for economic development. The American Economic Development Council has taken a leadership role in helping to strengthen the field of economic development. In its new publication *Economic Development Tomorrow,* the council defines economic development as follows: the process of creating wealth through the mobilization of human, financial, capital, physical, and natural resources to generate marketable goods and services. The economic developer's role is to influence the process for the benefit of the community through expanding job opportunities and the tax base. (*Economic Development Tomorrow,* 1991)

In today's global economy, economic competitiveness is driven by the wise use of technology and highly skilled employees. The global economy is increasingly becoming communications- and knowledge-based. Thus, the United States needs increased development and application of technology and improved levels of education in the workforce to remain competitive.

A major product of education, a skilled workforce, is increasingly being linked to quality economic development. "Labor is the key resource in the United States on which future competitive advantage will be based— not undifferentiated labor (brawn), but skilled labor (brains)" (American Economic Development Council, 1991, p. 16). In an information- and high-tech-based society driven increasingly by communication rather than transportation technologies, an increased educational level of the workforce is required.

One of the alternatives for improving the skills of the American workforce is to better use community colleges. Tom Peters, in an address to the Leadership 2000 convention in 1989 in San Francisco, said that the community colleges are America's primary hope in the race to remain competitive in the global economy. Community colleges have a history of more than four decades of directly supporting economic development through vocational education and contract education. The global economy requires new approaches to support economic development.

To illustrate the importance of the global economy to local economic development and the critical role community colleges play in their communities, the Montovan story is both unique, inspiring, and yet commonplace in a nation of increasing numbers of small businesses. Five years ago, the Montovans operated a small, struggling, family-owned business, which coincidentally was located across the street from Chaffey College's Center for Economic Development (CED). Through assistance from the CED staff in the areas of export trade and business operations, today the Montovans operate out of a new, much larger store and food processing plant. Their market niche is the food tastes of the people from the Pacific island cultures. Their business has increased at least fivefold, whether measured in productivity, profit, or employees, and they have been recognized as the small business of the year, locally and statewide.

The global economy will require not only greater use of technology but also new forms of working, which will themselves require more education. A greater emphasis on teamwork, collaborative planning and problem solving, and partnerships will require significant improvements in the human relations skills of employees.

Traditional Economic Development Activities of Community Colleges

Historically, community colleges have contributed to the local economy in several basic ways. These include deriving direct economic benefits from a college's presence in a community (employees are consumers of goods and services and pay taxes), preparing students to enter the workforce, improving basic skills of employees through remedial education, providing the first two years of education for professionals, offering business-specific courses, creating bridges from education to the world of work through various types of internships and cooperative education, providing prescreening services for employment, and offering placement services for both student employees and graduates. Community colleges also were involved with customized training from the time various federally supported manpower development programs were instituted. For the most part, federally supported training programs such as the contemporary Job Training Partnership Act were operated outside the primary mission of community colleges.

In 1982, Dale Parnell, then president of the American Association of Community and Junior Colleges (AACJC), now AACC, provided the leadership for the creation of what was to evolve as a new kind of partnership. The Association of Community College Trustees (ACCT) joined with AACJC in sponsoring public and private, labor and management, education and employer partnerships to focus on the importance of human resource development to the broader process of economic development. The Putting America Back to Work project later became known as the AACJC/ACCT Keeping America Working Project and attracted a great deal of support and public attention. The Sears Roebuck Foundation provided major funding for the program. Four types of partnerships were targeted in the project strategy for community colleges: (1) business, industry, labor; (2) public employer; (3) small business; and (4) high school and college (American Association of Community Colleges, 1985).

The Keeping America Working project was an excellent demonstration project that showed the capability of community colleges in responding to the needs of employers. Feedback from those involved in the partnerships, on all sides, was very positive. The project became a catalyst for many state and local training projects, supported in a variety of ways all across America.

Contemporary Economic Development Programs and Activities in Community Colleges

All across America, more than thirteen hundred community colleges are responding to the need for involvement in local economic development efforts. These approaches range from the building of separate and distinct facilities for supporting economic development to various programmatic responses. Several factors have coalesced to move economic development to the forefront of community colleges, encouraging partnerships and resource sharing. These conditions include an increasingly competitive global economy that requires a more highly educated workforce; a more competitive market economy, forcing the private sector to operate with fewer resources and greater expectations of their employees; continued tax resistance from the public, thus decreasing the funding available to government at all levels, including the public institutions they support; and the introduction of sophisticated technology into the workplace, thereby creating the need for greater teamwork, not only between individuals but also between manufacturers, suppliers, and distributors.

Community colleges have long played a role in supporting economic development in their communities, even when it was not referred to as economic development. What is different today is the major influence of the global economy. This larger, intrusive environment forces all local organizations to think globally while acting locally. The changing and increased standards for the workforce are generating a great deal of pressure on education to be more productive.

The economic development function of education requires a different approach. Economic development is an extension of the institution into the community being served. It is usually accomplished through the development of partnerships with business, industry, and government. These partnerships enhance the relationship between the community and the institution and generate a positive and participative aspect to that relationship. Nowhere is this more in evidence than in the area of job training and retraining, which is essential to a business's growth and competitiveness. Today's educational institution's role in job training and retraining is quite different than in the past because the training and retraining needs of business have become much more critical. Rapid response to a specific deficiency in a business may be vital to the business's survival.

In addition to education and training, educational institutions have another very important role to play in economic development—that of business expansion and retention. States are spending millions of dollars to entice companies to relocate. Educational institutions are the primary choice of businesses to meet their needs, but if an institution does not have the educational response capability, businesses increasingly take on the responsibility to do their own training or retraining.

Reaching out to business, industry, and government by providing a variety of educational and training opportunities is the educational institution's way of reciprocating in partnership development. These partnerships with educational institutions again help to define the role that educational institutions play in economic development.

In the past, the faculty in educational institutions were viewed as an intellectual resource to the communities in which they worked. This resource was generally accessed by the community through requests for speakers, advisory committee participation, and consultation. In terms of economic development, these intellectual resources are accessed to help solve problems in business, industry, and government, especially in terms of business expansion and retention. Not only does this benefit those being served, but it provides an avenue whereby faculty can develop relationships with business, industry, and government and use their expertise in program development, curriculum review, job training sites for students, job shadowing for faculty, internships, mentoring, and endless other areas of importance to business, industry, government, the educational institution, faculty members, students, and the community.

Another very important benefit derived from partnerships is the knowledge each partner gains from the other. Examples of this include specific employee-employer educational and training needs, as well as teacher and training program needs, including equipment and monetary support. Direct involvement with business, industry, and government provides the unique opportunity to understand fully the future workforce needs in the new and emerging technologies and what changes an educational institution should make in student, program, and faculty preparedness.

In 1989, Margaret Thomas of the Midwest Research Institute prepared *A Portfolio of Community College Initiatives in Rural Economic Development* for the U.S. Department of Commerce (Thomas, 1989). The report surveyed more than two hundred rural-area colleges. The study of economic development activity in rural community colleges is crucial to understanding the comprehensive role of all community colleges in economic development for several reasons: approximately half of all community colleges nationally are rural; in many rural settings, few resources exist for promoting economic development beyond the local community college; and in rural communities, it is much easier to identify the community and therefore to measure the college's contribution to economic and community development.

The primary findings of Margaret Thomas's research were the following: the college president or board of trustees must take the initiative to commit the college to a greater role in economic development; public awareness is critical because it legitimizes the program; colleges must foster an understanding that program staff will generally depart from the typical academic faculty profile; linkages with traditional economic development organizations are critical; tapping existing resources, particularly local resources, must be an early and continuing function of the development effort; and successful programs used a wide variety of funding sources.

Studying community college involvement at the local level reflects a great deal more diversity and therefore provides a much richer understanding of the range of local economic development activities in which community colleges are involved. Economic development programs in community colleges are not transportable. Each community college must study the communities in its district, form relationships with community leaders, and through discussion and mutual planning develop the unique programs that fit the local community's needs and assets.

Community colleges can significantly increase their contributions to the economy through regional and state consortia. For example, in California a small amount of state funding created the California Community Colleges' Economic

Development Network (ED>Net), which has enjoyed a great deal of success in supporting employers. The mission of ED>Net is to link California's 106 community colleges for quick response to support California's economic growth and global competitiveness. ED>Net, begun in 1988, sponsors collaboratives of colleges in focused areas of service, referred to as *initiatives*. All 106 community colleges are involved in at least one of the nine initiatives. There are ten centers for international trade development, fourteen small business development centers, eight centers for applied competitive technologies, six regional health resource centers, ten workplace learning centers, five advanced transportation technology centers, and twenty-seven colleges that have adopted the environmental technologies program initiated by ED>Net. In 1994–95, these initiatives, excluding the environmental technologies programs, provided assistance to more than fifty thousand clients.

Recent success stories include the development of a highly successful small business to teach Spanish to U.S. bankers, insurance executives, hospital employees, and farmers. The company was established through Bakersfield College's Small Business Development Center, which provided assistance in start-up efforts, business planning, and tax and licensing requirements of small business owners. And in partnership with a local community college, a Los Angeles defense contractor was able to successfully respond to the challenges of recent defense cutbacks by refocusing its strategic directions into new commercial opportunities. Total quality management training provided by West Los Angeles Community College was a key influence in establishing a new direction for this company. Obviously, the community colleges, through ED>Net, are making a difference in their local communities (ED>Net, 1996).

In a 1991 study of 151 selected American community colleges conducted by the author, it was confirmed that training, in a variety of forms, is the primary contribution community colleges are making to economic development. It was also found that programs to assist employers with quality and productivity are relatively new activities community colleges are offering. There is an increasing emphasis on technology that includes high-tech training, technology transfer, technology resourcing, and computer applications.

Conclusion

A review of community college practices in economic development suggests better public policy is needed at all levels of government, as well as improved coordination of policy affecting and enabling economic development. Mechanisms that ensure a higher level of protection of the economic development process from political intrusions are also required to support more long-term processes for improvement. In the absence of such protection, programs that clearly benefit the public are sometimes abandoned after a great deal of investment and before a return on the investment can be realized.

The following recommendations are made in the spirit of improving economic development, a process that is of vital interest to all Americans in a highly competitive global economy. The recommendations focus on the role community colleges can play in this process.

- Ongoing research needs to be done on the actual involvement of two-year colleges in economic development, with a focus on the full potential of these 1300 institutions networked across America to support local economic development and to identify the barriers to their participation. A key research activity is to establish discussion forums that assemble community college and university leadership to discover common areas of interest and opportunities for collaboration. These types of discussion formats also can result in a valuable information source for research purposes.
- A system of model programs, established on a competitive basis, should be funded by federal, state, or local governments as a mechanism to test the full potential of community colleges in assisting their local communities with economic development. Of consideration might be AACC's leadership in an organized effort to obtain such support from community-focused agencies such as the Kettering Foundation.
- Partnerships are essential as a way of maximizing benefit while reducing duplication of effort and enhancing cost effectiveness. The entire range of potential partnerships needs to be cataloged and the advantages and disadvantages of each partnership identified. Using today's accessible technologies, a core group of community colleges can develop a centralized information source using the Internet. This source can link available training and technical assistance with community business and training needs nationwide. A similar approach is the ED>Net Home Page (http://ednet.cc.ca.us), which offers complete descriptions of ED>Net initiatives, contact sources, and project descriptions.
- One of the natural areas of support by community colleges is that of small business. The Small Business Administration has encouraged such a role for community colleges, but more needs to be done by both state and local governments. Community college administrators would be well served to develop close relationships with state and local officials and corporate and civic leaders, not only to ensure that local business interests are addressed but also to assume the role of a broker of services between business owners and public assisted programs and resource areas.
- Although training is the area where community colleges are making their biggest contribution, in a knowledge- and communication-based global economy, a great deal more needs to be done, especially in the area of partnerships with employers. By working closely with chambers of commerce, community colleges can easily identify new and existing businesses that may require specialized training. This is particularly true for businesses that are directly affected by changing environmental conditions such as defense cutbacks, technological shifts, and a multicultural global economy.
- The area that seems most fertile for future involvement of community colleges in economic development is community development. Community

development provides a common meeting ground for discussion, collaboration, and formal partnerships among community colleges; utilities; economic development professionals; city, county, and state officials; and the private sector. Again, taking a leadership role in facilitating ongoing, collaborative discussions among community leaders, private and public, is a key activity community colleges can pursue to demonstrate their commitment and to provide opportunities for assisting their local communities.

- Because of the high-quality, unique relationships community colleges have with their local communities, the colleges can serve in a variety of mediator roles to facilitate local problem solving and development. This is an area needing research to document the activity of the colleges and explore possible ways of expanding this role. In fact, there is general agreement that social conditions often play a major part in local economic development efforts. Community colleges can expand their role by working closely with local schools, community assistance groups, civic organizations, and parent groups to sponsor education or training activities that address social concerns: youth development, substance abuse prevention, or welfare-to-work.
- More information is needed from existing databases, such as those maintained by the U.S. Department of Commerce, to indicate economic activities and trends by state and regions. This data could be a baseline component of assessment by community colleges in responding to local economic and community needs and with proper adaptation could be incorporated into the Internet-based shared information systems previously described.

References

American Association of Community Colleges. *Responding to the Challenge of a Changing American Economy.* Washington, D.C.: American Association of Community Colleges, 1985.

Macomb Community College. *Critical Issues Facing America's Community Colleges.* Warren, Mich.: Macomb Press, 1992.

American Economic Development Council. *Economic Development Tomorrow.* Rosemont, Ill.: American Economic Development Council, 1991.

Deegan, W. L., and Tillery, D., and Associates (eds.). *Renewing the American Community College: Priorities and Strategies for Effective Leadership.* San Francisco: Jossey-Bass, 1985.

ED>Net. "World Wide Web Home Page." [http://ednet.cc.ca.us]. Apr. 1996.

Koepke, R. L. (ed.). *Practicing Economic Development.* Rosemont, Ill.: American Development Council Educational Foundation, 1991.

Thomas, M. G. *A Portfolio of Community College Initiatives in Rural Economic Development.* Kansas City, Mo.: Midwest Research Institute, 1989.

JERRY W. YOUNG is superintendent and president of Chaffey Community College in Rancho Cucamonga, California. He has served on the executive committee of the California Community Colleges' Economic Development Network for the past four years and served as the group's co-chair for three years.

*As an emerging profession, economic development has standards of
professionalism that are still not completely defined. Demands for
recognition and expectations of greater accountability are leading to
necessary improvements in training and performance.*

Professionalizing the Economic Developer

Mark D. Waterhouse

Ask one hundred economic developers how they got into the field, the old
adage goes, and ninety-five will tell you: by accident. As with many such
adages, there is a great deal of truth to this one. For many working in the field,
this was not their profession, vocation, or intended career—it was merely a
job. This is obviously not a sound basis for expecting relevant pre-employment
training or the commitment of time and funds to obtain training after employment, when the duration of that employment frequently is minimal.

Compounding this problem, the relatively small size of the group
employed in economic development has led to almost no undergraduate programs in the field and very few graduate-level programs. Further, local-level
politicians, who are responsible for much of the hiring (read: political appoint-
ment) of economic developers across the country, have historically not realized
that the skills of their economic developers should be similar to those of their
town planners and city engineers. The times, they are a-changing.

Emergence of a Profession

The economic development profession has evolved from a loosely, often unde-
fined occupation to its current recognizable status. Even with significant
progress, however, economic developers must continue to engage in self-
assessment to ensure that their academic and job skill preparation will ade-
quately meet the profession's constantly changing requirements.

Historical Background. Economic development, in very simple terms, is
the process of businesses finding locations from which to generate marketable

NEW DIRECTIONS FOR HIGHER EDUCATION, no. 97, Spring 1997 © Jossey-Bass Publishers

goods and services. (For a more official definition of economic development, see Swager, 1991, p. 3.) As a process, it has existed since the first business found its first location. As a practice where individuals and organizations have attempted to assist in the process in order to influence where that business location would occur, economic development (more often called *industrial development* in earlier days) only traces back to the second half of the nineteenth century, when railroads and electric utilities established departments to attempt to attract new businesses into their service territories. Given no prior demand for such services, no one had any particular preparation for doing the job.

In the early twentieth century, local chambers of commerce or boards of trade entered the arena in order to represent their communities. By the mid-1920s, a critical mass of industrial development programs across the country led to the establishment of the American Industrial Development Council—AIDC (now the American Economic Development Council—AEDC) in 1926. A key purpose of this organization has been to upgrade the skills and proficiency of those engaged in the practice of industrial and economic development. Despite this effort, economic developers still suffered from an image bordering on that of charlatans and snake oil salesmen well into the second half of this century. In 1963, an AIDC request to a national foundation for financial assistance "was summarily dismissed with the comment that 'the practice of industrial development was categorized as little more than hucksterism and piracy'" (Handley, 1995, p. 12).

At this same time, the first national effort to train economic developers was under way. Started by the Southern Industrial Development Council (SIDC) and operated by the University of Oklahoma's College of Continuing Education, the first Industrial Development Institute was offered in 1962. Shortly thereafter, SIDC "suggested that the sponsorship be given to the American Industrial Development Council and the university to give the program a national focus" (Thompson, 1995, p. 74). Over a thirty-year period, this program—now called the Economic Development Institute (EDI)—has grown continually to the point that in 1993 a special section of *The Wall Street Journal* on executive education listed EDI as the second most popular public-enrollment executive education offering ("Executive Education," 1993).

A Changing Mind-Set. After nearly one hundred forty years, the practice of economic development is evolving into a legitimate profession—at least, its practitioners think so. "If, as Webster defines it, a profession is 'a vocation or occupation requiring advanced education and training,' then we are a profession somewhere between infancy and adolescence" (Waterhouse, 1995, p. 2).

Yet there has been a noticeable shift in mind-set about how those in the field of economic development define *profession* and *professional*. Where once we thought of our profession as "a vocation or employment, a whole body of persons engaged in an activity," we now believe we are engaged in "a calling requiring specialized knowledge and often long and intensive academic preparation." Similarly, as professionals, we have evolved from merely "participating for financial gain or livelihood in an activity or field of endeavor" to believing that we really are professional, and as such are "characterized by or conforming to the technical or ethical standards of a profession, engaged in one of the learned professions" (Swager, 1991, p. 28).

A key concept in defining a profession is academic preparation. Economic developers are buying the message that it no longer makes sense to try to fly by the seat of the pants with only on-the-job training. Attendance at AEDC-accredited educational programs clearly demonstrates this trend. From the first basic industrial development course established in Texas in 1967, these entry-level offerings (now called *economic development courses* or *EDCs*) have expanded to twenty programs educating approximately one thousand students annually and are offered at universities such as the University of North Carolina-Chapel Hill, Texas A&M, Ball State University, Southern Illinois University, and the University of South Florida. Similarly, from the first entering class of thirty-nine at the inaugural Industrial Development Institute, this program has grown to an average of approximately three hundred entering the program each year.

Key Characteristics of the Economic Development Profession

For the neophyte or outsider, the practice of economic development may look fairly simple—some good people and communication skills, some knowledge of marketing techniques, and an enjoyment of public visibility. Oh yes, and a high threshold of frustration and tolerance of nonsuccess. Beyond these, however, there are two defining characteristics of the profession.

Interdisciplinary Skills. Very few professions require the mixture of skills necessary for successful economic development. Certainly not all economic developers use them all every day, nor can developers be equally expert in all areas. They must, however, have more than just passing familiarity with all the skills and certainly must know where to find experts in areas where their own knowledge is weak.

What are these skills? A list in no order of priority includes computers and office technology, engineering and construction, communications (both written and verbal), research and statistics, economics and economic geography, human relations and management, education and workforce development, financing, real estate, international relations, marketing, law, government, planning (both community and strategic), business administration, and entrepreneurialism.

From a different perspective, skills necessary for economic developers can be categorized as leadership skills (communicating, planning, decision making, serving on boards, consensus building and group dynamics, and delegation); theoretical skills (globalization of the economy, general development theories, and specific economic development strategies); practical skills (computers, management, sales, and grant writing); political skills (understanding mission, funding sources, those who provide oversight and direction, competing agencies or groups, and allies, and knowing how to build and capitalize on networks and take credit when it is deserved); and change skills (becoming a lifelong learner, being willing to give up past ways of doing things, and keeping abreast of current events) (Thomas, 1995).

Constant and Rapid Change. The second defining characteristic of economic development is change. One need only look at the application of technology to see the effects on the economic development process and practice. Over the past two decades, economic development offices have had to add computers, faxes, modems, cellular phones, video marketing (now being replaced by computer diskettes and CD-ROMs), geographic information systems (GIS) capabilities, and home pages on the World Wide Web in order to stay competitive in the field. Technology, through both downsizing from automation and the proliferation of home-based offices, is having major effects on both employment and space needs, two primary concerns of most economic developers. Economic developers do not make these trends happen; they cope with them.

Similarly, during these same two decades, economic developers have had to learn about the service and global economies, impact fees, super-lien laws, incentive clawbacks, and a myriad of other new terms and concepts. Although economic developers may have little idea what the next wave of changes will be, they know they are inevitable and that they must constantly upgrade professional skills to survive.

Increasing Demands for Professional Recognition and Professionalism

Establishing a successful career as an economic developer presents many challenges. By recognizing these challenges, the profession has taken a proactive approach to increased recognition and acceptance.

Economic Development's Dark Side. Many economic developers are tired of having to lead a nomadic existence in order to find adequate compensation. They are equally tired of the lack of job security stemming from the fact that so many positions in the field are subject to the winds and whims of politics. Surveys of economic developers and their spouses since 1990 have found significant concerns about long work hours, the necessity of changing jobs every three to four years (either for advancement or from necessity), low incomes, low net worth, the threat of income loss, low job satisfaction levels, burnout, and similar issues (Devine, 1995).

Mounting frustration from these situations, coupled with increased intention to make economic development a long-term, if not life-long, vocation, have reached a critical point where those in the profession are beginning to take steps to protect themselves. This includes taking a proactive role in policy formation, rather than merely reacting to policies after they have been created by others. More important, however, is an increased awareness of the necessity of upgrading skills through continuous education. One indicator is a gradually increasing number of attendees returning to the Economic Development Institute on a post-graduate basis. Another is the popularity of a current presentation on how to negotiate employment contracts. The bottom line is that economic developers are tired of living "on the dark side" and are increasingly demanding recognition and taking action to demonstrate that they are members of a legitimate profession.

Accountability. Such recognition is not happening and should not happen automatically. There is a trade-off at work. In exchange for professional recognition, customers, stakeholders, and funding sources are requiring better performance and greater accountability. A current dilemma is determining how to objectively measure and evaluate economic development performance.

A recent study from the W. E. Upjohn Institute for Employment Research (Bartik and Bingham, 1995) concludes that although it is possible to evaluate economic development programs, most such efforts measure activity (that is, they are quantitative in nature) rather than accomplishment or effect (a qualitative approach). Economic developers know this situation is a risky one and, in 1991, went on record as recognizing that "if there is a single, most important challenge to our profession and professionalism as we go forward into the 1990s, it may be the development of effective and acceptable methods and measures of our performance and impact" (Swager, 1991, p. 33).

As a result, AEDC's Preeminence Task Force has identified two critical performance indicators for the organization. The first is creation of the industry-standard model for evaluating economic development projects based on a return on investment. The second is creation of the industry-accepted model for documenting the value-added benefit and return on investment of an economic development professional in a community (Weddle and Ramey, 1995).

Professional Responses and Initiatives

There are many other examples of ways in which individual professionals and the profession collectively are attempting to demonstrate improved capabilities and performance.

Improved Planning and Management. Until recently, it was not unusual for economic development organizations to be budget-driven rather than planning-led. The basic theory was that you plotted and schemed to obtain the largest possible budget, and then once you knew what the number was, you figured out how you were going to spend whatever was left over after you paid yourself (and your staff, if you had one) a reasonable salary. Besides being a poor management method, heightened expectations of accountability no longer allow this approach.

Economic developers have had to learn strategic planning techniques and apply those lessons in managing a process that results in specific accomplishments. Even further, they must actually implement the plan and compare their performances with schedules and milestones. What initially was considered cumbersome, bureaucratic, and too time-consuming has now become a standard and ongoing management tool for most economic developers. A second wave has emerged, adding a preliminary round of strategic visioning that is intended to result in a plan driven by intent rather than by just currently available resources.

Both courses and publications on effective economic development planning are now necessities for professional development and organizational libraries. Strategic planning is a core element of the curriculum shared by the twenty economic development courses across the nation. The Economic Development Institute follows up with advanced strategic planning and a major core course titled "Community of the Future Principles," which teaches how to guide an effective community visioning process. At the local level, college and university resources are frequently used in the strategic visioning and planning process, particularly in a facilitation role.

The Quality Imperative. Not even economic development can escape total quality management (TQM). As clichéd as many consider the topic to have become, it is difficult to argue with the concept of consciously working to improve the performance of economic development organizations. Whether it is called *building the high-powered organization* or simply *doing the right things right,* better customer and stakeholder service and more effective resource use have become essential to the demonstration of economic development professionalism. AEDC's *Economic Development Review* devoted an entire issue to the topic (Koepke, 1993), and the Economic Development Institute offers courses. Higher education institutions can play a key role in helping local economic development programs with quality improvement.

Improved Research Capabilities. As might be expected with any emerging profession, prior research and publications have been somewhat limited until recently. Since its 1962 inception, the Economic Development Institute has included a thesis requirement, intended in part to add to the body of literature about the field. Despite the obvious weakness that younger professionals may lack the experience to select and research important and emerging topics, the EDI Thesis Library contains a wealth of important information.

Beyond this, however, are increased opportunities for economic developers of all levels of experience and responsibilities to publish in a variety of professional journals. Perhaps the three most widely read are AEDC's *Economic Development Review,* Sage Publication's *Economic Development Quarterly,* and the National Council for Urban Economic Development's (CUED) *Commentary.* Among these three, professionals now have available nearly one thousand pages a year of new information, approached from both the practitioner and academic perspectives.

In a new initiative, the AEDC Educational Foundation has recently allied with Cleveland State University to establish an Economic Development Research Institute (EDRI). The purpose of this institute is to identify topics that economic developers need to be more proficient professionals, to identify means for conducting the necessary research, and to widely disseminate the results. Once again, this is an effort started by economic developers because they recognized it as an important tool for enhancing professional skills and knowledge base. As EDRI develops, it will likely form a model for facilitating cross-institutional collaboration in addressing challenging research needs.

Certification and Accreditation. There are many professional certifications related to economic development (planning, finance, research, to name a few—and many economic developers are obtaining these cross-disciplinary certifications), but there is only one certification for economic development generalists, AEDC's *Certified Economic Developer* designation. Established in 1970, more than eleven hundred economic developers have attained the CED (or the predecessor, CID) designation, and approximately six hundred fifty are currently certified. A bright spot for the future is increasing interest in obtaining professional certification as indicated by rising participation in the examination process and as expressed as an intention by students attending the Economic Development Institute.

On the other hand, it is somewhat troubling that there are only six hundred fifty CEDs, if there are indeed somewhere between twelve and fifteen thousand economic development organizations in the United States (a conventional wisdom estimate that cannot be attributed to any particular source) and approximately three thousand such organizations with professional staffs (Boyle, 1995), many with multiple professionals. In part this is because the designation has not clearly demonstrated specific value to those who hold it. In turn, this reflects a lack of appreciation by those who hire and set the salary scales, as well as the nature of economic development professionalism, and how it can be recognized. This is a chicken-and-egg situation, where the CED designation has not yet attained the critical mass to clearly demonstrate its importance. Nor will it attain that critical mass and importance until more people are motivated to obtain the designation.

A new initiative, AEDC's Accredited Economic Development Organization (AEDO) program, looks at organizational preparedness and ties together many of the aspects of professionalism previously considered. Organizations that desire an outside appraisal of organizational deficiencies and advice on how to correct them can request an audit. Those that believe they have no serious weaknesses can apply for official accreditation. Organizational evaluation considers such things as the existence of strategic management and marketing plans, availability of trained and experienced staff, and similar indicators of professional excellence.

Code of Ethics. Part of the dictionary definition of a professional relates to conformance with ethical standards. Although AEDC has had published standards of conduct since its inception, the membership and leadership concluded two years ago that an eighty-one-word statement was no longer adequate to describe ethical expectations in today's complex business and political world. As a result of considerable research of thirty-two existing codes of ethics from other professional organizations and a survey of sixty economic developers concerning their experience and concern with ethical dilemmas, AEDC has recently adopted a much more detailed code. This code covers eleven topics but concentrates on the key areas of confidentiality, truthful communications, and conflicts of interest. One of the eleven topics reads as follows. "Members will endeavor to perfect themselves in their economic development profession to the best of their ability as an opportunity to serve their clients and our collective society." Prior to adoption, the importance of having an updated code was described in this fashion: "If AEDC is to be recognized as a preeminent organization, it will be important that its members are seen not as self-centered, opportunistic individuals, but rather as major contributors to the well-being of others than themselves" (Foden and Worrell, 1995, p. 77). The same can be said for the economic development profession in general.

Defining the Body of Knowledge. A weakness with the knowledge base of any emerging profession is that no systematic attempt has been made to identify the essential components of that knowledge base. The situation holds an even greater possibility for problems when multiple organizations are involved in defining that knowledge base. For example, the course directors of the twenty economic development courses work regularly to establish an agreed-upon core curriculum, the Economic Development Institute's Curriculum Committee meets annually to review and revise the EDI curriculum, and AEDC's Certification Board manages the CED examination procedure, including selection of the topics and questions included on the examination. Without a concerted effort to interrelate instruction and examination, there is the risk, perhaps even the likelihood, that teaching and testing will be covering different topics.

For that reason, a task force was established in 1993 to provide coordination among the various entities leading to a better definition of the economic development profession and the critical body of knowledge that should be covered in both effective economic development instruction and relevant economic development examination (Wansley and Oilschlager, 1995). This task force has led to a broader effort to better define the purposes and intended customers of each program, leading to shared understanding and agreement on the core courses, key topics, and teaching objectives of each program. This coordinated and cooperative effort, expected to be completed by late 1996, cannot help but improve both portions (teaching and testing) of the professional development program. In addition, it is likely that additional educational needs will be identified and cannot be met within the current framework of training programs. These will provide a ready-made list of program needs to which higher education institutions may respond.

Professional Challenges on the Horizon

The practice of economic development is not universally accepted as a necessary endeavor. There are those who argue that economic development is really a zero-sum game and that economic developers add nothing to the overall economic pie. Left to their own devices, companies will find suitable locations without the help of economic developers, who, as some believe, spend large sums of money and other resources interfering in the free-market economy. Competition between neighboring communities or states, which would occur naturally as companies compare potential locations, is exacerbated by the runaway use of incentives to sway deals and sometimes steal companies.

Economic developers pride themselves on the numbers of new jobs they create and increases in capital investment, which translate into increased tax revenue. Others see increased traffic congestion; pressures on schools, utilities, and other services affected by growth; loss of green space; and other changes in the historic personality of communities—all caused by economic developers. Economic developers are agents of change. That is an extremely important responsibility and one that must be pursued in the most professional manner.

How do we do it? How do we enter the field and perform effectively? How do we adapt to changing trends, tools, pressures, and expectations? How do we develop the desired recognition of ourselves as professionals and our endeavors as a profession? How do we survive and succeed?

Education! Pick your adjective: constant, continual, lifetime, never-ending. At one end of the spectrum, new opportunities must be created for precareer training at the undergraduate and graduate levels. There is evidence that this is already occurring, and ongoing research through the AEDC Educational Foundation is documenting existing and planned economic development courses (Iannone, 1995; Swager, 1995). Preliminary research has identified forty-eight colleges and universities with some kind of degree or credit instruction in economic development. The vast majority of the offerings (66 percent) are at the level of a formal track or a specialization or concentration within some other general degree such as planning, geography, economics, finance, or management. Similarly, 66 percent of the offerings are at the master's level, but only 9 percent are at the bachelor's level (Swager, 1996).

The primary reservation by colleges and universities about establishing a bachelor's-level economic development curriculum is that the field is too small to justify the resources necessary to create a new program. In other words, the demand to be an economic developer does not justify supplying the education. This argument was made in a major "Tenth Anniversary Essay" in the *Economic Development Quarterly*. A strong counter-argument, however, is that the interdisciplinary training required for an economic development degree or major is already available. A student can use an interdisciplinary approach if the course work has direct relevance to other fields such as commercial banking, commercial and industrial real estate, public administration, real estate and commercial lending law, and other occupations. Although a new overview course covering the theory, principles, and jargon of economic development may be necessary, other courses (which already exist at many colleges and universities) comprising the core of a major would include offerings in economics, marketing, finance, public administration, small business development, real estate principles and practices, and environmental issues.

As earlier noted, a significant weakness of the profession has been the necessity for most new economic developers to obtain relevant education once established in the field. Colleges and universities, most of which spend a great deal of time talking about the important role they play in economic development, have neglected a primary responsibility in facilitating undergraduate-level education. A creative approach using existing courses and recognizing much broader applicability than just the economic development field provides a ready solution. Western Connecticut State University is currently establishing an economic development major based on exactly this approach and justification.

Until the field can clarify its direction sufficiently, much of the entry level training will occur, perhaps appropriately, as a continuing education activity. And it is at this end of the spectrum that we find an increasing need for more and better continuing education opportunities. There is a role for both colleges and universities and the professional organizations. Old topics must be taught to new professionals. New topics will continue to emerge and must be taught to everyone. New instructional methods must be employed to reach those who cannot come to fixed location offerings. The Connecticut Community-Technical College System is currently working with the Connecticut Economic Resources Center to create a five-course training and team-building program for all the state's economic developers, leading to designation as a certified lead manager. This program allows greater use of a new electronic database and communications system and provides the state with a fully trained professional economic development team.

Colleges and universities looking for assistance in identifying economic development educational needs, designing practical and effective programs, and locating qualified instructors can generally find an economic development professional association within their states by contacting the state department of economic development or commerce. In addition, five primary national and regional economic development associations, all of which run active educational programs, are presented in the resources list at the end of this chapter.

Certainly, many initiatives are already under way to improve the level of professionalism in economic development, but the aspect of education is of paramount importance. This field is information intensive. Information is the economic developer's currency. Information can be obtained either haphazardly or through preplanned, intensive, short course, or institute approaches typical of continuing education offerings. Education is the key to improved professionalism in economic development, and successful economic developers constantly seek such learning opportunities. Those who do not will struggle or fall by the wayside. Those in the education business have a responsibility to help economic developers make the right choice. Those in the economic development business have the responsibility to make it.

References

Bartik, T. J., and Bingham, R. D. *Can Economic Development Programs Be Evaluated?* Kalamazoo, Mich.: W. E. Upjohn Institute for Employment Research, 1995.

Boyle, M. R. *Economic Development Organizations Survey Report.* Growth Strategies Organization, 1995.

Devine, J. A. "The Dark Side of Economic Development." *Economic Development Review,* 1995, *13* (3), 62–66.

"Executive Education." *The Wall Street Journal,* Sept. 10, 1993, pp. R1–R14.

Foden, H. G., and Worrell, A. N. "Toward a Code of Ethics for AEDC." *Economic Development Review,* 1995, *13* (3), 77–79.

Handley, G. "Responding to the Challenge of Professional Development: The Programs of AEDC." *Economic Development Review,* 1995, *13* (3); 12–15.

Iannone, D. T. "Economic Development Education: Future Developments and Directions." *Economic Development Review,* 1995, *13* (3), 31–35.

Koepke, R. L. (ed.). *Economic Development Review.* Theme: Total Quality Management, 1993, *11* (3).

Swager, R. J. (ed.). *Economic Development Tomorrow: A Report from the Profession.* Rosemont, Ill.: American Economic Development Council, 1991.

Swager, R. J. "'Professionalization' of Economic Development: The Higher Education Linkage." *Economic Development Review,* 1995, *13* (3), 75–76.

Swager, R. J. *The Status of Degree-Granting Programs in Economic Development.* Interim Progress Report to the AEDC Educational Foundation, Jan. 1996.

Thomas, J. R. "Skills Needed by the Economic Developer." *Economic Development Review,* 1995, *13* (3), 9–11.

Thompson, N. "The Economic Development Institute." *Economic Development Review,* 1995, *13* (3), 74–75.

Wansley, J. D., and Oilschlager, K. H. "Defining the Profession." *Economic Development Review,* 1995, *13* (3), 70–71.

Waterhouse, M. D. *American Economic Development Council News.* Annual Report Supplement, Apr. 1992, p. 2.

Weddle, R. L., and Ramey, D. "AEDC 2005: Shaping a Strategy for the 21st Century." *Economic Development Review,* 1995, *13* (3), 16–19.

Additional Resources

American Economic Development Council
James Ahr, CAE, President
9801 West Higgins Road-Suite 540
Rosemont, IL 60018-9944
(708) 692-9944

Mid-America Economic Development Council
Dorothy Collins, Executive Director
P.O. Box 7130
Deerfield, IL 60015-7130
(708) 317-0035

National Council for Urban Economic Development
Jeffrey A. Finkle, Executive Director
1730 K Street, N.W., Suite 915
Washington, DC 20006
(202) 223-4735

Northeastern Industrial Developers Association
Paul J. Hockersmith, CED, Executive Director
P.O. Box 968
Elkton, MD 21921
(410) 620-1965

Southern Economic Development Council, Inc.
Nancy C. Windham, Executive Director
229 Peachtree Street, Cain Tower, Suite 1008
Atlanta, GA 30303
(404) 523-3030

MARK D. WATERHOUSE is a certified economic developer and is president of Garnet Consulting Services, Inc. He is past chair of the American Economic Development Council, served as dean of the University of Oklahoma's Economic Development Institute from 1989 to 1993, and is executive director of the Northeastern Industrial Developers' Association.

Institutions of higher education are well positioned to assume key roles in shaping economic development of the future. Recognizing these roles and developing a strategic response is the challenge for continuing higher educators.

Strategies for the Future: Continuing Higher Education and Economic Development

James P. Pappas, Cynthia M. Eckart

Numerous opportunities are emerging for continuing higher education to shape future economic development activities. In fact, some might conclude that the future is already here. Institutions of higher education are indeed shaping economic development, often under the auspices of federally funded initiatives, which have created such programs as one-stop workforce assessment centers and school-to-work transition programs through the U.S. Department of Labor; community outreach partnership centers through the U.S. Department of Housing and Urban Development; promotion of dual-use technologies through a consortium of the U.S. Departments of Commerce, Defense and Energy, NASA, and the National Science Foundation; and comprehensive educational centers designed to bring systemic change to K–12 education through the U.S. Department of Education. All of these program initiatives will improve or change many of our nation's core activities (education, technology application, workforce training, urban development). And, perhaps more significant, all will equip our nation to compete in a global economy.

In the context of this volume, a rather critical aspect of the aforementioned programs is that many are being conducted by innovative segments of higher education in partnership with federal agencies and other public or private organizations. In fact, higher education often serves as a linking mechanism to assemble the resources required to carry out such federal initiatives. Grossman writes that "perhaps the most powerful force for economic change in the nation is the ability to marshal the resources of the private sector and

NEW DIRECTIONS FOR HIGHER EDUCATION, no. 97, Spring 1997 © Jossey-Bass Publishers

government to form collaborative partnerships" (1994, p. 25). It is an out-growth of such thinking that we introduce one of the significant opportuni-ties for continuing higher education to shape economic development of the future.

Preparing for the Future

Various authors in this volume have provided several examples of the poten-tial roles for higher education in supporting economic and community devel-opment. Each brings a unique perspective from the context of the originating institution, the geographic region, and the participating partners. The model described in the following section reflects another example of an institution's unique contribution to economic development. More important, however, are the implications it demonstrates for higher education.

Partnership 21: a model for the future. The University of Oklahoma's College of Continuing Education has served as an education, training, and research partner with the Federal Aviation Administration (FAA) for more than twenty-four years. During this time, both organizations have experienced several tran-sition periods in the field of aviation, culminating in a collaborative partnership to address the future challenges of the industry. Through continued network-ing with agency representatives, the university learned of the FAA's long-term initiative to harmonize aviation standards around the world. In an increasingly global economy, the safety and quality of aviation systems have become of utmost importance. By working closely with nations around the globe, the FAA hopes to achieve a common standard for the world's aviation systems.

As a result of the university's experience in aviation-related research, edu-cation, and training (global positioning satellite research, graduate engineer-ing courses in composite materials, air traffic controller training), the agency requested assistance in formulating plans for a series of international aviation symposiums. The symposiums were targeted for specific regions of the world and were designed to discuss existing aviation conditions and to determine what could be done to connect countries' needs with available resources in the United States. Much of the expert knowledge and resources were available from agency staff and FAA aviation contractors, some of the largest corpora-tions in the world. However, because of federal regulations and current pro-fessional obligations, it was impossible for agency personnel to serve as consultants to other nations. In addition, as a federal contracting agency, it was prohibitive for the FAA to broker business ventures on behalf of current or potential contracting firms.

The University of Oklahoma, as a neutral third party, was able to overcome these limitations. The university's College of Continuing Education proceeded to work with the agency to design the first of a series of Partnership 21 sym-posiums. The primary objective of Partnership 21 is to encourage a coopera-tive alliance among the FAA, participating countries and regions, academe, private-sector aviation or supplier companies, and associations to jointly develop a seamless global aviation system for the twenty-first century. A key aspect in planning the event was securing industry sponsorships from aviation corporations. Again, the university's third-party status allowed the institution to work closely with aviation contractors to encourage their support of this high-profile, international event.

The first Partnership 21 event was conducted at the University of Oklahoma's Oklahoma Center for Continuing Education and attracted senior civil aviation officials from thirty-five western hemispheric nations. As reflected in the comments of an FAA administrator, "this symposium links countries from the Arctic to the Antarctic with U.S. businesses, universities, and federal agencies to cooperatively pursue common interests to ensure the highest quality standards for the aviation industry" (Hinson, 1994). The event was jointly designed and conducted by the university, the FAA, and aviation industry sponsors, which included Motorola, Martin Marietta, Fluor Daniel, LB&M, Inc., United Airlines, and American Airlines. Director-generals and civil aviation officials from South, Central, and Latin American nations as well as Canada and Cuba were provided the opportunity to exchange expertise about common visions for both a standardized global aviation system and the current status of participating nations' aviation infrastructures (airport facilities, aircraft, aviation workforce) and systems (air traffic control systems, weather systems).

Event partners were then able to direct visiting officials to the resource expertise required for modernization assistance. A subsequent result of this event was the development of business alliances between participating countries and U.S.-based aviation industries. Examples of spin-off business activities include a survey of all Category II aircraft runways throughout Latin America, aviation infrastructure development in Venezuela, and airport modernization efforts in Brazil, Columbia, and Uruguay.

A second Partnership 21 symposium was conducted in the fall of 1995 in Dubai, United Arab Emirates (UAE). This event targeted countries of the Middle East (Bahrain, Kuwait, Oman, Qatar, Saudi Arabia, Lebanon, Jordan, United Arab Emirates) and such neighboring North African nations as Algeria, Egypt, Ethiopia, and Morocco. Once again, the university worked in partnership with the FAA, Honeywell, Inc., Lockheed Martin, and the Gulf Cooperation Council to develop a two-day event focusing on aviation applications of Global Positioning System satellite technology. Partnership 21 not only served as a way to share technical expertise and predict future activities in the region but also generated new business opportunities for trade practices among U.S. corporations and participating nations. Examples include the facilitation of long-term purchase agreements of U.S. aircraft as well as the purchase of navigation and communication systems by Middle Eastern countries. In addition, the purchase and installation of Global Positioning System equipment for transportation needs other than aviation were direct results of contacts developed at the symposium.

The third Partnership 21 event, scheduled for the summer of 1997, will also be conducted in Dubai, UAE for aviation officials from the Middle East and Africa.

The decision was made to return to Dubai because of the Dubai International Air Show, which would attract participants; the desire of the UAE to be a sponsor; and the need to deal with safety problems experienced by airlines in that region. The program will focus on the safety issues and related infrastructure and equipment needs of the represented countries. More than fifty potential aviation firms have been targeted to serve as sponsors, participants, and presenters. In addition to previous Partnership 21 sponsors, examples include Northrop Grumman, Motorola, Bechtel, Morgan Stanley, Chase Manhattan, Citicorp, Boeing, and Rockwell International. Through Partnership 21, decision makers responsible for building their countries' aviation infrastructure will have the opportunity to gain a better understanding of how to incorporate U.S. products and services into their development plans (Federal Aviation Administration, 1996).

Partnership 21 represents one of many similar opportunities for continuing higher education to broker resources in order to facilitate economic development opportunities on a local, national, and international scale. The contributions of events like Partnership 21 are threefold. First, it serves as a mechanism with which to link service and product suppliers with purchasers, thus stimulating trade and business exchange. Second, it establishes a neutral forum in which senior executives can discuss the most current trends or technologies that will affect the economic future of their nations. And third, the University of Oklahoma's facilitative role in the Partnership 21 series not only makes this activity possible but also opens new contacts and opportunities for the institution to pursue with nations around the globe.

Replicating a similar event requires an institution to seek collaborative opportunities among business, government, and education. Often, this can be accomplished through current relationships by recognizing future trends and developing alliances that will capitalize on predicted conditions. The following are important aspects to remember when designing these types of programs, whether international or domestic, large or small.

- Ensure that the roles of the institution and other partners are clearly established. This requires a mutual recognition of the unique contributions of each and should include both practitioner and academic elements.
- Identify event sponsors that reflect a variety of constituents, particularly those with technological expertise, an applications focus, and a grasp of the political elements of the topic.
- Remember that the credibility of the event is often centered on the ability to attract planning partners, cosponsors, and program speakers (politically as well as technically sound), all of whom are recognized and respected by the participating audience.
- Aim for all partners to gain something from the event—new business opportunities, increased networking, visibility, information dissemination, political

positioning—and recognize that the motive for each sector (industry, government, education) will be different.

Implications for Higher Education

Given the Partnership 21 example and other case studies provided throughout this volume, one can now examine the strategies higher educators should consider to strengthen their role in shaping future economic development. As clearly demonstrated by the scenario in this chapter, institutions are uniquely positioned to serve as neutral, third-party facilitators or brokers of information. This role requires an institutional capability to proactively seek and establish linkages among university faculty, staff, and external (local community, state, national and international) resource expertise. Key to accomplishing this role must be the institution's demonstrated commitment to outreach as well as a continued appraisal of environmental, business, and economic conditions.

For example, to assemble sponsors for Partnership 21, the University of Oklahoma and industry representatives worked closely with the FAA to determine the topics of immediate concern to specific geographic regions. This joint environmental analysis led to the identification of industry sponsors whose technical expertise and applications experience would be of greatest benefit to participating countries.

As a broker of resources, higher education should also assume a visionary leadership role for the future. Institutions are responsible for the creation and dissemination of knowledge and research technologies, the latter often done in partnership with corporate or publicly funded research and development labs. Essential to economic development is the dissemination of practical, application-based technology or knowledge. As a leader, higher education can assist others to adapt to changing economic conditions that in reality are often shaped by the application of knowledge and research. The University of Oklahoma's participation in Partnership 21 not only demonstrates a commitment to advanced aviation systems but also validates the institution's cutting edge role in aviation technology, education, and training. Involvement in this event has led to increased recognition from international nations and subsequent business contacts both for the university and for local industries and business development agencies.

The Oklahoma Department of Commerce is now working with the university to pursue cooperative training and language programs with Vietnam. ATIS, Inc., an Oklahoma aviation consulting firm, is working to establish an air cargo airline between Bolivia and the United States and is developing aircraft inspection training for the countries of Aruba and Ecuador. The University of Oklahoma has expanded its aviation-related training to Russia and is discussing a collaborative internship with several airlines that were conference partners. These represent but a few of the secondary spin-off activities that can result from these types of events and often lead to tertiary activities of the future.

Finally, assuming an active leadership role in economic development provides an opportunity for institutions to create new revenue opportunities in a time of diminishing public resources. For many, this represents a stronger outreach approach to respond to the needs of constituent audiences and a movement from revenue dependency to revenue generation. Partnership 21 required a significant institutional commitment to assume responsibility for an event of high international profile and the financial support of multinational corporations. The event's success was dependent on an institutionwide effort, not only for logistical purposes (facilities, security, media) but also for establishing the credibility that was needed to attract international aviation officials and presenters. This was achieved not by university efforts alone but rather through the collaborative efforts of event partners. The university's revenue opportunities from Partnership 21 will be long-term in nature. However, the institution has successfully positioned itself to meet the assessment, education, and training needs that will likely follow aviation technology and infrastructure advancements of participating countries.

Higher education is well positioned to be a central player in economic development and in fact is already performing this function, as indicated by the many examples presented in this volume. What continuing higher educators must do is reevaluate institutional commitments to outreach and begin to develop a collaborative strategy to assume one or perhaps several roles in supporting future economic development.

References

Grossman, H. J. "Business-Education Partnerships and Workforce Development." *Commentary*, 1994, *8* (1), 24–29.

Hinson, D. Comments from opening address of Partnership 21 Symposium, University of Oklahoma, Norman, June 1994.

JAMES P. PAPPAS is the vice provost for outreach and distance education and dean of the College of Continuing Education at the University of Oklahoma.

CYNTHIA M. ECKART serves as assistant to the vice provost for outreach and distance education at the University of Oklahoma.

INDEX

Ordering Information

NEW DIRECTIONS FOR HIGHER EDUCATION is a series of paperback books that provides timely information and authoritative advice about major issues and administrative problems confronting every institution. Books in the series are published quarterly in Spring, Summer, Fall, and Winter and are available for purchase by subscription and individually.

SUBSCRIPTIONS cost $52.00 for individuals (a savings of 35 percent over single-copy prices) and $79.00 for institutions, agencies, and libraries. Standing orders are accepted. New York residents, add local tax for subscriptions. (For subscriptions outside the United States, add $7.00 for shipping via surface mail or $25.00 for air mail. Orders *must be prepaid* in U.S. dollars by check drawn on a U.S. bank or charged to VISA, MasterCard, or American Express.)

SINGLE COPIES cost $20.00 plus shipping (see below) when payment accompanies order. California, New Jersey, New York, and Washington, D.C., residents, please include appropriate sales tax. Canadian residents, add GST and any local taxes. Billed orders will be charged shipping and handling. No billed shipments to post office boxes. (Orders from outside the United States *must be prepaid* in U.S. dollars by check drawn on a U.S. bank or charged to VISA, MasterCard, or American Express.)

SHIPPING (SINGLE COPIES ONLY): $20.00 and under, add $3.50; to $50.00, add $4.50; to $75.00, add $5.50; to $100.00, add $6.50; to $150.00, add $7.50; over $150.00, add $8.50.

ALL PRICES are subject to change.

DISCOUNTS FOR QUANTITY ORDERS are available. Please write to the address below for information.

ALL ORDERS must include either the name of an individual or an official purchase order number. Please submit your order as follows:
  Subscriptions: specify series and year subscription is to begin
  Single copies: include individual title code (such as HE82)

MAIL ALL ORDERS TO:
  Jossey-Bass Publishers
  350 Sansome Street
  San Francisco, California 94104-1342

FOR SUBSCRIPTION SALES OUTSIDE OF THE UNITED STATES, contact any international subscription agency or Jossey-Bass directly.

OTHER TITLES AVAILABLE IN THE
NEW DIRECTIONS FOR HIGHER EDUCATION SERIES
Martin Kramer, Editor-in-Chief